To each and every one of the peeps who have
supported me on my journey so far, this is for you.
Love rules and so do you!

DINNER EXPRESS

Fast, easy dinners (+ hacks!)
for busy people

George Georgievski

plum. Pan Macmillan Australia

CONTENTS

Introduction

Family means everything to me, and some of my best childhood memories are of my mum, dad, sister and me sitting around the dinner table. We'd discuss how many times I had gotten in trouble at school that day or my dad would tell us something funny that had happened to him at work ... it was super awesome.

Back in the day, my mum was a factory worker, so she'd be home by 3.30 pm and would usually spend an hour or two preparing dinner. We had the best times during those magic hours and, when we were lucky enough, my mum would even whip up a dessert or cake. This time together gave me an appreciation for food and for the family stories behind the meals that my mum would cook. There were a lot of 'when I was your age' discussions and it was also a great time to drop birthday present hints, some times more successfully than others (I still haven't forgotten the year I asked for Adidas runners and instead got cheap knock-offs).

Fast forward to the next generation. My wife Marina and I both work full-time, and we have often struggled to find the time to recreate that special bonding time of our childhood dinners. Our time at home during the week is scarce, with after-school activities for Anela and Kiki taking up most nights. I wanted to work out a way to ease the dinnertime pressure, to make this time as relaxed and golden as it was during my childhood.

There's no chance I can cook the dinners that my mum used to make back in the day, I just don't have that amount of time. So I've worked out shortcuts and other ways to take inspiration from my mum's cooking and the special memories I have of dinnertime, to make it work in the context of our busy, modern lives.

I've designed the recipes in this book to take the stress out of your evenings and help you get a fresh, healthy and delicious dinner on the table – one that your family will actually want to eat! Most can be whipped up in 30 minutes and some are even quicker (look for the 'Ridiculously fast!' symbol throughout the book).

You can also customise any of the recipes to suit your family's preferences. For example, I've used microwave rice throughout the book, but if you have a little more time, you can cook your rice from scratch. The pies and pastries all use puff or filo pastry from the freezer and come together in no time, and there are loads of ideas for including veggies in your dinner in a way that kids will love. I've also devoted a whole chapter to creating an impressive meal using a supermarket roast chook and just a few extra ingredients (the Portuguese Grilled Chicken on page 113 is a personal favourite).

And because I couldn't write a book without including some awesome lunchbox inspiration for both you and your kids, I've included a month of lunches to give you some new ideas for how to use your leftovers from dinner the next day.

I've been lucky enough to travel around the world and try lots of interesting foods and flavours, and I've taken inspiration from many different countries when creating these recipes. I'll never forget getting ripped off in the South of France with my best mate Waz, paying 50 euros for a couple of sausages, or trying street food in Cambodia that changed the way I approach cooking curries. I'll also never forget eating my grandmothers' soulful food in Macedonia. Food is my life and I've been eating since 1973, so I know my sh#t. Lol.

I really hope this book helps to bring you and your family together for dinner, especially during the week. I believe it's an opportunity to enhance our conversation, connection and communication. There is nothing better than watching your family eat well and connecting with each other over a meal – it's truly special. Take these recipes and make them work for you to create some fun memories. Peace out.

George

'Better put a lock on this lunchbox at work! I've included a month's worth of lunchbox inspiration throughout the book. Time to say goodbye to boring sandwiches.'

Fast-track your dinners!

TOP TIPS TO SAVE YOU TIME & EFFORT

Here are my top ideas to help ease the burden of the daily dinner grind. All it takes is a bit of planning and dinners will become a breeze!

Plan your dinners before you shop

My family used to be shocking at deciding what to eat for dinner. When someone suggested a meal there was always an objection. I realised that I needed to change tack, so I reached for my favourite cookbook and some sticky notes, handed them to Kiki, Anela and Marina and asked them to pick two dinners each. I made a list of all the ingredients, along with any modifications, such as removing walnuts for Anela's nut allergy. When I went to the supermarket I only bought the ingredients on the list instead of randomly buying produce to fill the fridge. The results? Bang! Dinner for the week was sorted.

Batch cooking rules

Being a parent is taxing and you don't want to spend every evening in the kitchen, so cook a double batch of a meal that you know the whole family loves and that keeps well (I'm not talking fresh salads here!). You can have it again later in a few days' time or freeze half for next week.

Love your freezer

Most cooked foods can be frozen for at least a month, and I love taking out a frozen curry before I leave for work in the morning, knowing that all I need to do is zap it in the microwave when I get home. Lots of the pies and pastries in this book, such as the Cheat's Ricotta and Feta Burek (see page 53) and Veggie-loaded Sausage Rolls (see page 47), freeze well, as does the Chill-out Con Carne (see page 149). I also love making big batches of my favourite sauces, such as Satay Sauce (see page 122) and Teriyaki Sauce (see page 116), and then freezing them in portions for a later date.

Shortcuts are okay!

You don't always have to create meals from scratch. Check out Pimp Up Your Roast Chicken (see page 109) to see how easy it is to make ten incredible meals with a supermarket roast chook. Making your own marinades can be fun and if you've got the time, go for it, but don't be afraid to buy store-bought marinades and sauces. Shortcuts can actually be a cool way to discover new flavours.

Prep ahead

Make life easier by prepping your veg when you get home from the shops. I give all my produce a wash and store it in plastic containers in the fridge so that it's ready to use throughout the week. You can also make many of the dressings and sauces in this book a few days ahead and store them in sealed jars in the fridge until you're ready to use them.

Order online

I have to admit that I am a supermarket addict (I often go three times a week), but if you're short on time, why not shop online? Ordering online saves time, especially if you get it delivered, which means your weekends will be free to hang with family and friends.

Look for bargains

I love it when the supermarket catalogue drops in my letterbox. The most expensive items on my shopping list are meat, chicken and fish, so when I see premium beef mince on sale, I'll buy loads, divide it into portions and freeze. Just remember to take it out the night before to defrost!

STOCK UP ON ESSENTIALS & SAVE TIME!

The key to whipping up sensational dinners in 30 minutes is to keep your kitchen stocked with all the right things. These are the essential ingredients that I keep in my freezer, fridge and pantry at all times so that I can always create quick and healthy meals my family will love.

Frozen puff and filo pastry

The most used ingredients on my social pages. There are so many insanely delicious dinners you can create if you've got a supply of puff and filo pastry in your freezer. Turn to the Pies, Pastries & Breads chapter on page 41 for ideas.

Mince

Good ol' mince. It freezes well and can be easily divided into family-sized portions so you're never far away from a delicious meal. Head to the Mighty Mince chapter on page 139 and get planning!

Eggs, milk, cheese and butter

Few households are without these essential ingredients and for good reason. They bring flavour and depth to many meals. Try whipping up my Hidden Cauliflower Cheesy Fettuccine on page 19 and you'll see what I mean.

Bread, wraps and tortillas

I usually buy two loaves of bread and pop one in the pantry and one in the freezer. Wraps and tortillas have a good shelf life and you can use them to create meals like my Sneaky Veggie Quesadillas (see page 22) or Beef Burrito Cones (see page 173).

Dried pasta and noodles

I bet you've got some in your pantry right now! With dried pasta and noodles on hand, a quick and delicious meal is never far away. I've even included some recipes that make use of everyone's favourite 2-minute noodles! See the Pasta, Noodles & Rice chapter on page 69 for ideas.

Rice

Stock your pantry with both regular and microwave rice (for those times when you really don't have time). I also occasionally use black or brown rice for a healthier option. You will find rice recipes dotted throughout this book.

Pantry produce

Onions, garlic, ginger, sweet potatoes and potatoes are all no-brainers for me. They store really well in the pantry, so you don't have to worry about them going limp in the fridge, plus there are so many meals you can make if you have these ingredients at your fingertips. My Mega-loaded Sweet Potatoes (see page 27) are an excellent place to start.

Canned stuff

I always keep my pantry stocked with canned tomatoes and beans (such as kidney and cannellini). The more the better in my opinion, especially considering they usually only cost $1 each. Stock up the next time you go to the supermarket and you've got dinner in the can (ha!). Many of the recipes in this book use canned produce – check out my Chill-out Con Carne (see page 149) and Pirinska 8 (Macedonian baked beans with meatballs; see page 158).

Olive oil

I'm European, so what can I say? Whether it's for salad dressings or to cook with, you need olive oil in your pantry at all times as an easy way to add incredible flavour to even the simplest of meals.

Vinegars

Red wine, white wine and balsamic vinegars are always on the shelf in my pantry. Mixed into a salad dressing, they bring any green leaves to life. See Ten Salad Dressings that Totally Rock on pages 30–1 to get inspired. And don't forget to save your used jars!

Sauces and marinades

Everyone has tomato sauce at home, but I also love to have mustard (great for dressings), mayonnaise and my favourite marinades. Hoisin sauce is also a must – it's great for Asian-inspired meals such as my Sticky Pork Noodles (see page 150).

Flour

I always have plain and self-raising flour in my pantry. Self-raising flour is great for whipping up the Speedy Pizza Dough on page 50.

Spices

In my spice rack you'll find: salt flakes, black pepper, smoked paprika, cayenne powder, garlic powder and onion powder. Cayenne powder might be too spicy for your little ones, but the others are all real crowd-pleasers and will add heaps of flavour to your meals.

EQUIPMENT THAT WILL MAKE YOUR LIFE EASIER

Some kitchen equipment is non-negotiable in my book. The following tools will save you both time and energy in the kitchen, which are crucial when it comes to making quick weeknight dinners.

Sharp knife

No one touches my knife and I love it. I sharpen it regularly and use it for everything. Yes a good knife is expensive, but it's reliable and makes me feel like a chef every time I use it. Invest in at least one good knife.

Kitchen scissors

I couldn't live without my kitchen scissors, especially when I need to divide a whole roast chook for dinner. They make the task so much easier – see page 111 for instructions.

Chopping boards

I have at least a dozen chopping boards at home. I also use them as serving platters, so I get good use out of them. Wooden chopping boards are best, but don't forget to seal them with a dab of vegetable oil every now and then, to stop them drying out and cracking. Avoid putting them in the dishwasher, too.

Frying pan

You need at least one large heavy-based frying pan that retains heat well. When it comes to cooking a good steak or stir-frying veggies over high heat, a solid frying pan will give you great results every time.

Air fryer

Although all of the recipes in this book can be made without an air fryer, if you want to save time these machines are the best! You don't need to preheat them, they cook food quickly and make everything crisp and delicious while using a minimal amount of oil.

Stainless-steel mixing bowls

Most recipes involve mixing of some sort or another. Stainless-steel bowls are cheap and usually come in sets with multiple sizes, meaning you don't have to keep washing up the same bowl. They're used in commercial kitchens a lot so they must be good, right? Just avoid mixing anything acidic, such as lemon juice or vinegar, in metal bowls as the metal can react with the acid and affect the flavour of your food.

Protein shakers

C'mon, we all have at least three or four in the cupboard somewhere, right? I use my protein shaker every single day to make pancake batters, cake mixes, waffles, muffins, sauces and marinades. They make washing up a breeze and you're less likely to make a mess on the kitchen bench.

Used jars

Instead of chucking empty jars into the recycling, give them a wash and keep them on hand to shake up your salad dressings. It's fast and mess free, and you can store the leftover dressing in the fridge for another night. See pages 30–1 for my favourite jar dressings.

Airtight containers

After a shopping spree I wash all my berries and pop them in an airtight container. They stay fresher for longer and are ready for snacking or putting in the kids' lunchboxes. I also rest my doughs and pastry in them – it works a treat.

Microplane

You probably already own a cheese grater, but my tip is to buy a microplane. They are super sharp and make quick work of grating ingredients such as garlic, ginger and parmesan. I have a small handheld one and it rocks.

Metal peelers

Just like you need a good knife, you also need an awesome metal peeler. Plastic ones tend to only last a few months, but metal peelers are cheap and sturdy.

Metal tongs

Just buy a heap. They tend to break easily but they're a necessity, especially for tossing salads, lifting pasta out of the cooking water and into the sauce, and grilling food on the barbie.

Measuring cups and spoons

These are cheap and make prepping your ingredients a breeze.

Garlic press

Not only does a garlic press prevent your fingers smelling of garlic for hours, it also saves you time compared with finely chopping it with a knife.

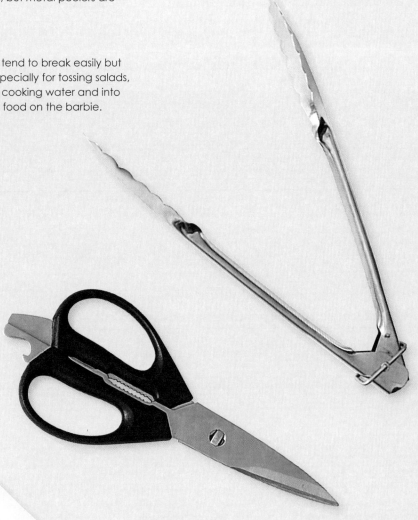

Vegetable dishes that you (and your kids) will actually want to eat!

SALADS & HIDDEN VEGGIE HACKS

'Even the sharpest little detectives won't be able to find the cauliflower hiding in here.'

HIDDEN CAULIFLOWER CHEESY FETTUCCINE

Ridiculously FAST!

What I love about melted cheese is the fact that it takes over the taste of everything else you might have in a dish. Introducing the hidden cauliflower in my cheesy fettuccine! It's easy and cheesy, and will change the way you make mac 'n' cheese, too. Let's go.

SERVES 4

What you'll need

250 ml (1 cup) milk
60 g butter
125 g (1 cup) grated cheddar
½ teaspoon freshly ground black pepper
3 tablespoons grated parmesan
1 tablespoon plain flour
300 g packet of cauliflower rice
500 g dried fettuccine

It's time to do this

Bring a large saucepan of salted water to the boil.

Meanwhile, place a large frying pan over medium heat and add the milk, butter and cheddar. Let it melt away, stirring occasionally, and ensure that it doesn't boil. Add the pepper, parmesan and flour and keep stirring until the sauce looks silky and smooth. Add the cauliflower rice and stir through to soften.

Cook the fettuccine according to the packet instructions, then, using a slotted spoon, lift the pasta out of the boiling water and add it to the cauliflower cheese sauce. Add a couple of tablespoons of the pasta cooking water to thin the sauce a little and mix it all together. Serve straight away.

Did you know?

You can use any pasta shape here – my girls loved macaroni and penne when they were little, but the older they get the more they like different shapes such as fettuccine. Go figure!

Feel free to add other hidden veggies, or try different cheeses. I have also made this using blue cheese but my girls hated it, so approach with caution.

WONTON RAVIOLI WITH SECRET VEGETABLES

Ridiculously FAST!

Okay, what the actual? The title is confusing, but it's just my dad way of getting my girls to eat vegetables by hiding them in ravioli and smothering everything in a delicious tomato sauce. I discovered wonton wrappers about a year ago and now I use them all the time to make dumplings and filled pasta. When making this recipe, think about all the creative ways you can use the wrappers and the different veggies you can secretly add.

SERVES 4

Go grab this stuff

400 g microwave mixed vegetables
1 teaspoon salt flakes
2 tablespoons olive oil
½ onion, finely diced
1 teaspoon crushed garlic
400 g can crushed tomatoes
200 ml vegetable stock
20 wonton wrappers
2 tablespoons grated parmesan

Now do this

Microwave the veggies according to the packet instructions, then transfer to a bowl and add the salt and 1 tablespoon of the oil. Use a fork to mash the veg to a mashed potato consistency.

Bring a large saucepan of salted water to the boil.

Next, grab a frying pan and heat the remaining oil over medium heat. Add the onion and garlic and cook for about 5 minutes, until soft, then add the tomatoes and vegetable stock and bring to a simmer.

While the sauce simmers away, let's assemble the wonton ravioli. Pop a wonton wrapper in the palm of your hand and add about 1 tablespoon of your veggie mix. Using your finger, wet the edge of the wonton wrapper with a little water, then fold the wonton wrapper in half to form a rectangle and press the edges together to enclose the filling, making sure to press out any air bubbles. Repeat with the remaining wonton wrappers and veg.

Drop your ravioli into the boiling water and as soon they start floating to the top use a slotted spoon to transfer them to the simmering tomato sauce. Mix gently to coat in the sauce, then divide among shallow bowls, sprinkle the parmesan on top and start eating!

More stuff

Feel free to be as creative as you like with the wonton wrappers and make as many different shapes as you can think of: fold them in half at the corners to make triangles or use round dumpling wrappers to make semicircles. You can even get the kids to seal the ravioli with a fork.

Even though this is a fun dish, it's jam-packed with veggies. You can also add a tablespoon of essential vitamin powder to the mashed veg for an extra hit of goodness.

SNEAKY VEGGIE QUESADILLAS

Mexican food is a favourite in our house. My girls go nuts for it – all I have to say is 'Mexican' and they're high-fiving each other. This recipe is the bomb and perfect for midweek dinners as it's super quick and guaranteed to please. I've cooked these quesadillas in a chargrill pan to get fancy grill lines on them, but any frying pan will do the trick.

SERVES 4

What you'll need

1 tablespoon olive oil, plus extra for grilling
½ onion, finely chopped
1 red capsicum, finely chopped
2 chorizo sausages, finely chopped
1 tablespoon smoked paprika, plus extra if desired
1 teaspoon salt flakes
2 tablespoons tomato paste
250 g packet of microwave brown rice
425 g packet of corn cobbettes
1 avocado, diced
1 bunch of coriander, leaves picked
1 long red chilli, finely chopped (optional)
4 large soft flour tortillas
125 g (1 cup) grated cheddar
leafy salad, to serve
lime wedges, to serve

Rock it like this

Heat the oil in a frying pan over medium heat, add the onion, capsicum and chorizo and cook, stirring frequently, for about 5 minutes, until the chorizo is lightly browned. Add the paprika, salt and tomato paste and cook for 2 minutes.

Meanwhile, throw the rice and corn in the microwave and cook according to the packet instructions.

Add the rice to the pan, stir well, then add 125 ml (½ cup) of water and let it simmer for 8–10 minutes.

Meanwhile, grab another frying pan or a chargrill pan, coat it with a little olive oil, then cook the corn over high heat for about 2–3 minutes, or until charred to your liking. Set aside.

In a small bowl, mix the avocado with some of the coriander leaves and a little extra smoked paprika, if desired. Set aside.

Once your rice mixture is done, transfer it to a heatproof bowl and stir through the chilli (if using).

Wipe out the frying or chargrill pan, return to medium heat and add a tortilla. Spoon ½ cup of the rice mixture onto one half of the tortilla and top with 2 tablespoons of the cheese. Fold the tortilla over the filling and cook for 1 minute each side or until the cheese has melted. Repeat to make four quesadillas.

Serve with the corn, remaining coriander leaves, avocado, leafy salad and lime wedges.

Did you know?

I've served the corn alongside the quesadillas here, but if you want to get even sneakier with your veggies, slice the kernels from the cobs into the tomato and rice mixture.

You can replace the chorizo with beans for a meat-free version, but add extra paprika for that smoky flavour. Or try adding shredded cooked chicken for an extra protein hit.

Sneaky Veggie Quesadillas are perfect for lunch the next day. Check out the previous page for the recipe and don't forget to add some extra cheese for the win!

Got eggs? Got lunch! Simply hard-boil some eggs, halve them and place them on a bed of carrot spirals. Add your favourite fruit and veg and lunch is made.

MEGA-LOADED SWEET POTATOES

Sweet potato is the coolest veg. It provides healthy carbohydrates, and dressing it up with other delicious veggies is a win–win. I love coming home from work and dropping four sweet potatoes into the air fryer while I chill out and argue with the kids. This is another go-to lazy dinner that the family will absolutely love.

SERVES 4

Grab all of this

4 sweet potatoes
2 tablespoons olive oil
1 tablespoon salt flakes
1 teaspoon garlic powder
40 g salted butter
125 g (1 cup) grated cheddar
**400 g can mixed beans, rinsed
    and drained**
250 g (1 cup) natural yoghurt
425 g can diced beetroot, drained
**1 spring onion, finely sliced on
    an angle**

Time to get cracking

You can cook the sweet potatoes in the oven or an air fryer. If cooking in the oven, preheat it to 180°C.

Wash the sweet potatoes really well as we are going to leave the skin on. Rub the oil over the potatoes and season with the salt and garlic powder. If cooking in the oven, transfer the potatoes to a baking tray and cook for 40–50 minutes, until tender. If using an air fryer, cook at 180°C for 20 minutes.

Once the sweet spuds are ready, grab two forks and gently open them up along the middle to let all the steam out. Divide the butter among the potatoes and wait for it to melt, then top with the grated cheddar.

Place the mixed beans in a bowl and microwave on high for 3 minutes. Spoon the beans over the cheesy spuds and top with the yoghurt, beetroot and spring onion. Dinner's ready.

Extra awesome stuff

You can swap out the sweet potatoes for normal potatoes if you like. This recipe is all about encouraging kids to eat their veggies. As far as toppings go, you can add to or subtract any of the ingredients I've included – as long as you have butter and cheese everything will be fine.

THE BEST THAI BEEF SALAD

Ridiculously FAST!

There's only one thing better than eating this Thai beef salad, and that's having someone make it for you in Thailand. The first time I ate this I knew that the hero was the dressing. If you're not into beef you can easily swap it out for your favourite protein. Although there are a lot of ingredients, don't freak out. These flavours will be stage diving on your taste buds like Eddie Vedder during the *Ten* tour, early-90s style!

SERVES 4

What you'll need

- 2 tablespoons vegetable oil
- 3 x 250 g porterhouse steaks
- 1 tablespoon salt flakes
- 1 tablespoon freshly ground black pepper
- 2 baby cos lettuces, leaves separated
- 1 continental cucumber, halved lengthways, deseeded and sliced into half moons
- 12 mixed medley cherry tomatoes, halved
- ½ red onion, very finely sliced
- 2 tablespoons crushed peanuts

THAI DRESSING

- ⅓ cup mint leaves, finely chopped
- ⅓ cup coriander leaves, finely chopped
- 3 garlic cloves, crushed
- 2 tablespoons caster sugar
- 2 tablespoons fish sauce
- juice of 1 lime

Okay, let's get to it

Heat a large frying pan or chargrill pan over medium–high heat. Rub the vegetable oil over both sides of the steaks and season them with the salt and pepper. Place the steaks in the pan and cook for 3 minutes each side for medium–rare or until cooked to your liking.

While the steaks are grilling, grab a small bowl and place all the Thai dressing ingredients in it. Whisk until well combined, then set aside in the fridge for the flavours to infuse.

Place the lettuce, cucumber, tomato and onion on a large platter and toss well.

Remove the steaks from the pan and set aside to rest for about 5 minutes. Cut the steaks into 5 mm wide strips, then add them to the platter and toss together. Drizzle the Thai dressing over the salad and mix until the ingredients are well coated.

Scatter over the crushed peanuts and serve.

Bonus stuff

As I mentioned in the intro, you can use any protein you like, but if you use chicken you'll have to call it Thai chicken salad, lol.

If you want more carbs, spoon 1 cup of cooked microwave rice of your choice on the platter and top with the salad. The rice will absorb the dressing, making it a double win.

TEN SALAD DRESSINGS THAT TOTALLY ROCK

There is nothing quite like a freshly made salad dressing. They are super easy to make and taste so much better than any store-bought version. It's also heaps cheaper to make your own – you just need a few essential ingredients, such as olive oil, a couple of vinegars and your favourite mustards.

I have created ten dressings as a total dedication to Pearl Jam's first album, *Ten* (obvs).

Italian dressing

125 ml (½ cup) extra-virgin
  olive oil
2 tablespoons red wine vinegar
1 garlic clove, grated
pinch of salt flakes
pinch of freshly ground black
  pepper

French dressing

125 ml (½ cup) extra-virgin olive oil
2 tablespoons red wine vinegar
1 garlic clove, grated
pinch of salt flakes
1 teaspoon dijon mustard

Caesar dressing

3 tablespoons natural yoghurt
2 tablespoons finely grated
  parmesan
1 teaspoon dijon mustard
2 tablespoons extra-virgin
  olive oil
1 garlic clove, grated
2 anchovies, finely chopped
1 tablespoon lemon juice

Coleslaw dressing

125 ml (½ cup) extra-virgin
  olive oil
2 tablespoons white wine
  vinegar
1 tablespoon caster sugar

Honey–balsamic dressing

90 g (¼ cup) honey
2 tablespoons balsamic vinegar
1 tablespoon extra-virgin
  olive oil

Simple Asian-style dressing

2 tablespoons lime juice
2 tablespoons honey
80 ml (⅓ cup) sesame oil
1 tablespoon soy sauce
1 teaspoon finely chopped long red chilli
1 garlic clove, grated

Vietnamese dressing

125 ml (½ cup) water
3 tablespoons fish sauce
3 tablespoons rice wine vinegar
2 tablespoons lime juice
2½ tablespoons caster sugar
2 garlic cloves, finely chopped
1 teaspoon finely chopped long red chilli

Ranch dressing

90 g (⅓ cup) mayonnaise
2 tablespoons buttermilk
1 tablespoon white wine vinegar
1 garlic clove, grated
1 tablespoon snipped chives (or use dried)
1½ teaspoons smoked paprika

Lemon dressing

juice of ½ lemon
3 tablespoons extra-virgin
  olive oil
pinch of salt flakes
pinch of freshly ground black
  pepper
1 teaspoon dried oregano

Lochie T (aka honey–mustard dressing)

2 tablespoons extra-virgin
  olive oil
1 tablespoon red wine vinegar
1 tablespoon white wine vinegar
1 tablespoon balsamic glaze (see Handy
  Hints on page 32)
1 tablespoon mild American
  mustard
1 tablespoon honey
1 garlic clove, crushed
pinch of Vegeta stock powder

To make the dressings, place the ingredients in a jar, screw
on the lid and give it a good shake. Lightly dress your
chosen salad and toss to combine.

Leftover dressings will keep in the fridge for up to 1 week.

SMASHING PUMPKIN(S) SALAD

Okay, so now I'm singing the hit song 'Disarm' by the Smashing Pumpkins. A good pumpkin salad should always be three things: easy, delicious and loved by everyone. I have added goat's cheese instead of the usual feta, as I want the flavour of the cheese to be more subtle and creamy. Now let's get cooking.

SERVES 4

Stuff you gotta get

2 kg butternut pumpkin, peeled, deseeded and cut into 10 cm long slices

2 tablespoons olive oil

1 teaspoon salt flakes

1 teaspoon freshly ground black pepper

80 g (½ cup) pine nuts

400 g baby spinach

300 g cubed goat's cheese

Honey–Balsamic Dressing (see page 30)

balsamic glaze, to serve (optional; see Handy Hints)

Now the easy bit

Preheat the oven to 220°C and line two baking trays with baking paper.

Place the pumpkin in a large bowl, add the oil, salt and pepper and give it a good mix so the pumpkin is smothered in the oil. Tip onto the prepared trays and cook for about 25 minutes, until golden and cooked through. Set aside to cool.

Toast the pine nuts over medium–low heat in a small dry frying pan for 6–7 minutes, until golden brown. Keep the pan moving (if you're like me you will be flipping the pan about and spilling a few) or stir constantly, as the pine nuts can burn very easily. Transfer to a plate to cool.

Grab your fave platter, add the pumpkin, spinach and pine nuts and give it a little mix. Add the goat's cheese, but don't stress if it falls apart or crumbles as we can pass it off as being rustic. Drizzle the honey–balsamic dressing over the whole lot and finish with a drizzle of balsamic glaze, if desired.

Handy hints

The secret to this salad is the dressing, there's no doubt about it. I once made it with a mango curry dressing and I can safely say you don't need to try that. Feel free to experiment with the other dressings on pages 30–1 or add different ingredients to the salad. Before you swap out the pumpkin you need to come up with a good name for the salad, though.

Balsamic glaze is simply balsamic vinegar that has been reduced with a sweetener, such as honey or sugar, into a delicious gooey syrup. You can find it next to the balsamic vinegar at the supermarket. Give it a go!

'This salad rocks
Pearl Jam level.'

CHORIZO & GARLIC BREAD PASTA SALAD

What?! Garlic bread in a salad? Yep! Because we can. I love garlic bread – it's one of my guilty pleasures, so I had to figure out a way to enjoy it without the guilt. So I dropped it into a pasta salad already filled with delicious carbs, lol. I initially made this as a bit of a joke because my wife said I didn't eat enough salads. A couple of years later, this pasta salad is now on regular rotation in our household, and it's time to share it with you.

SERVES 4

Ingredients you'll need

- 1 small garlic bread baguette
- 500 g spiral pasta
- 1 chorizo sausage, very finely sliced
- 12 mixed medley cherry tomatoes, halved
- 15 mini bocconcini
- ⅓ cup basil leaves
- ½ red onion, very finely sliced
- Italian Dressing (see page 30)

Let's rock

Cook the garlic bread and spiral pasta according to the packet instructions. Drain the pasta and set aside to cool. Cut the garlic bread into cubes.

Heat a dry frying pan over medium heat and add the chorizo (you don't need any oil as the chorizo will release enough on its own). Cook for 5 minutes, until crisp, then use a slotted spoon to transfer the chorizo to a plate lined with paper towel to drain. Leave the oil in the pan over medium heat and add the garlic bread cubes. Toast for 3–4 minutes, until they absorb the delicious chorizo oil. Transfer to the plate with the chorizo.

Transfer the cooled pasta to a large serving bowl and add the tomato, bocconcini, basil leaves and onion. Toss through enough of the Italian dressing until the pasta is glistening, then add the chorizo and garlic bread croutons and toss again. Serve immediately.

Bonus stuff

If you can't find chorizo, feel free to use pancetta or bacon, cooked until crisp. You can also use whatever short-cut pasta you have in the pantry, or even try fresh egg pasta.

The salad dressing is a real winner in this dish – there's something so satisfying about making your own dressing. Check out my other dressings on pages 30–1.

This is perfect for work or school the next day, as the pasta continues to soak up the delicious flavours.

Turn an avo into instant guac! Simply remove the stone and lightly mash half the avo with a fork. Add some salt and pepper, top with tomatoes and coriander, and pop some corn chips into the lunchbox for dipping.

SPEEDY LAMB SALAD

Ridiculously FAST!

I was having dinner at my sister Suzy's place recently and I flipped out at her delicious lamb salad; in fact, I asked her to give me the recipe and she refused. After a few wines and a gin, she finally came round and dropped some subtle hints. I guess me begging for an hour probably helped, too. Lol.

SERVES 4

Go grab this stuff

300 g lamb backstrap

3 tablespoons olive oil, plus extra for rubbing

1 tablespoon salt flakes

1 teaspoon freshly ground black pepper

1 iceberg lettuce

1 Lebanese cucumber, halved lengthways, deseeded and sliced into half moons

200 g mini roma tomatoes, halved

1 yellow capsicum, sliced

50 g (½ cup) soft goat's cheese, cut into cubes

2 tablespoons balsamic vinegar

1 tablespoon balsamic glaze (see Handy Hints on page 32)

1 teaspoon dried oregano

It's time to do this

Let's start with the lamb. Rub olive oil over the lamb backstrap and season with the salt and pepper. Heat a large frying pan over medium–high heat, add the lamb and sear it for 3 minutes each side for medium–rare, or until cooked to your liking. Transfer the lamb to a plate, cover with foil and let it rest – it will continue to cook through and the juices will help marinate the meat.

Now the salad part. Break up the lettuce as rustic or as neatly as you like. Drop it in a large bowl and add the cucumber, tomato and capsicum. Carefully drop in the goat's cheese – it's a little difficult to handle as it's so soft, but it's way worth it.

For the dressing, grab a clean jar and add the oil, both types of balsamic and the dried oregano. Screw the lid on and give it a good shake, then pour the dressing over the salad and toss well.

Slice the lamb into 1–2 cm wide strips and place it on a chopping board to serve, so your peeps can help themselves. Place in the centre of the table with the salad and watch it disappear right before your eyes.

But wait, there's more!

The lamb backstrap is the secret to this recipe so I don't recommend swapping it out. If you're really lamb averse, you could use boneless chicken thighs at a pinch and adjust the cooking time.

I've gone a bit fancy here and topped the lamb with some oven-roasted rosemary sprigs and whole cloves of garlic.

Hearty bakes that will rock your world (because everything is better wrapped in pastry)

PIES, PASTRIES & BREADS

COBZZA

Who doesn't like an 80s-style cob loaf with a melted cheese fondu? Okay, I'm not really into it either, so I set myself a mission to make this retro classic super cool with a contemporary twist. I was thinking about it while eating pizza, then bang! It hit me. I'll create a cob-loaf dip with a pizza twist: cobzza!

My girls love pulling out the soft, inner bread and squeezing it to create edible bread balls, and when they're in the mood they even help fill the loaf with their favourite toppings. Make it a fun, interactive meal that everyone can participate in.

SERVES 4

Go get this stuff

1 x 25 cm round cob loaf
250 ml (1 cup) tomato pizza sauce
300 g (2 cups) grated mozzarella
12–15 slices of salami (hot salami totally rocks, just saying)
3–4 sprigs of basil, leaves picked
1 tablespoon extra-virgin olive oil
simple Italian salad, to serve (optional; see More Stuff)

Now what?

You can cook the cobzza in an air fryer or the oven. If cooking in the oven, preheat it to 180°C.

Using a bread knife, cut the top off the cob loaf – avoid the temptation to eat it as we need it later. Pull out most of the soft, inner bread from the cob loaf and set it aside, then press down on the hollowed-out base of the loaf to make a firm layer. This will prevent the ingredients from leaking through.

Spread half the tomato sauce across the base of the cob loaf, then top with half the mozzarella, half the salami and a few basil leaves. Drizzle half the olive oil over the basil leaves, then repeat the process until you've used up all the ingredients (save a few basil leaves for scattering over at the end).

Pop the reserved lid on top of the loaf. If cooking in the oven, transfer the cob loaf to a baking tray and cook for 20 minutes, removing the lid for the last 5 minutes of cooking to allow the cheese to get all melty and slightly grilled. If using an air fryer, cook at 170°C for 10 minutes, removing the lid for the last 3 minutes of cooking.

Top with the remaining basil leaves and serve with the reserved pulled-out bread for dipping into the cheesy sauce and a simple Italian salad on the side.

More stuff

Feel free to add any of your favourite pizza toppings. You can also make this cobzza with any style of bread, including sourdough, wholemeal and gluten-free bread.

To make a simple Italian salad, combine chopped lettuce, cucumber, tomato, red onion and a few bocconcini balls in a salad bowl and toss through some of the Italian dressing on page 30.

BRITISH FISH, CHIP & MUSHY PEA PIE

Okay, so this recipe is borderline crazy, but there is a story behind this madness.
A few years ago, I was in Manchester in the UK, rocking out at a show. I was really hungry
afterwards, so I asked a few locals to recommend the most British food there is, and the
most common reply was fish and chips with mushy peas. Unfortunately I ran out of time, but
I thought to myself one day I'm going to make my own Aussie version of this British classic.
So here we are, with some puff pastry, fish fillets and frozen peas. I'm bound to
get a few Brits hunting me down for this one, lol.

SERVES 4

What you'll need

2 potatoes, peeled and finely sliced
2 teaspoons salt flakes
300 g frozen peas
20 g salted butter
½ teaspoon freshly ground
   black pepper
1 sheet of frozen puff pastry,
   just thawed
4 x 100 g skinless boneless white fish
   fillets, such as whiting
80 g tartare sauce

It's time to do this

Preheat the oven to 180°C.

Place the potato in a large saucepan and cover with cold water.
Add 1 teaspoon of the salt, then bring to the boil over high heat.
Reduce the heat to a simmer and cook for 5 minutes. We are not
making mash so make sure the potato doesn't overcook, as we'll
be cooking it again in the oven later. Drain and set aside.

Meanwhile, grab another saucepan, fill it with water and bring to
the boil. Drop in the peas and let them boil for about 5 minutes,
until they float to the top. Drain the peas and return them to the
pan along with the butter, remaining salt and the pepper. Place
the pan over low heat and roughly mash the peas with a fork or
a potato masher thingy. Set aside.

Lightly grease four 11 cm ramekins. Cut the puff pastry sheet into
quarters and line each ramekin with a square of puff pastry. Prick
the bases with a fork, then divide the mushy peas among the
ramekins. Use your fingers to break up the fish and place it over
the peas – don't be afraid to load them up. Spoon the tartare
sauce over the fish.

Layer the slices of potato over the tartare sauce – be as fancy
as you like. Transfer the ramekins to the oven and cook for
20 minutes, until the potato is golden and the pastry has puffed
up over the sides of the ramekins – it will look super cool.

Handy hints

If you really love mushy peas, do what I've done here and
make double the quantity so that you have extra to serve
on the side.

VEGGIE-LOADED SAUSAGE ROLLS

Sausage rolls are an Aussie favourite but supermarket varieties aren't always the healthiest option, so I decided it was time to take control. This simple recipe is super fast, fun to make and the results are epic. Most sausage roll recipes show you a 45-minute step-by-step method on how to make a tomato sauce or relish. That ain't going to happen here – just grab a sauce bottle and squeeze. On weeknights I want my girls fed and showered, with their uniforms and bags ready for school the next day.

MAKES 8

Grab all of this

4 sheets of frozen puff pastry, just thawed
8–10 sausages (any flavour you like)
2 carrots
1 zucchini
1 teaspoon salt flakes
1 teaspoon freshly ground black pepper
1 egg, lightly beaten
1 teaspoon sesame seeds
½ teaspoon poppy seeds
tomato sauce, to serve
leafy salad, to serve

Let's rock

You can cook the sausage rolls in an air fryer or the oven. If cooking in the oven, preheat it to 180°C. Line a baking tray with baking paper.

Cut the puff pastry sheets in half. Now grab your favourite sausages and snip the tops off. Squeeze the contents out along the middle of each pastry sheet – it should run the length of the pastry; if it doesn't, add a little extra filling from another sausage.

Grab your veggie peeler and peel long strips of carrot and zucchini. Place a couple of strips of each vegetable over the sausage meat, then add a pinch of salt and pepper. Here is the fun part. Working with one pastry sheet at a time, flip the pastry over the filling, then use a fork or your fingers to seal the pastry edges together.

Place the sausage rolls on the prepared tray, seam-side down, and brush with the egg. Sprinkle over the sesame and poppy seeds; you can even score the pastry if you want to get fancy.

Cook the sausage rolls in the oven for 20 minutes. If using an air fryer, cook at 180°C for 10 minutes.

Serve with a side of tomato sauce and a leafy salad. Nailed it!

Extra awesome stuff

You can also use vegan sausages for a meat-free alternative, but don't squeeze the 'meat' out! Simply place the sausages on the pastry and top with the veggies.

Feel free to hide as many veggies as you like, just don't tell any of your little peeps.

Make several batches of these sausage rolls and pop the uncooked rolls in an airtight container in the freezer for up to 3 months. Just remember to let them thaw out first before cooking.

Is there anything better than leftover pizza for lunch the next day? Turn to the next page for my super speedy pizza recipe that can be whipped up in less than half an hour.

These sausage rolls are filled with hidden veg and are so much better for you than the supermarket variety! Take a look at the recipe on the previous page to see just how quick and easy they are to make.

PUMP-UP-THE-BASE PIZZAS

I have, hands down, the best pizza dough recipe. But it's a two-day process that requires yeast, expensive flour and a bit of patience. I needed to come up with something faster but that still delivered on taste. Behold my pump-up-the-base pizzas! They are quicker to make than ordering a pizza, and a fraction of the price, too.

MAKES 2

Grab the following

80 g tomato paste
150 g (1 cup) grated mozzarella
2 garlic cloves, crushed
20 thin slices of salami
2 teaspoons extra-virgin olive oil
2 tablespoons grated parmesan
basil leaves, to serve

SPEEDY PIZZA DOUGH

300 g natural yoghurt
500 g (3¼ cups) self-raising flour,
  plus extra for dusting
1 teaspoon salt flakes
1 tablespoon extra-virgin olive oil

Okay, let's get to it

Crank your oven to maximum heat (this is usually 250°C). Lightly flour two large baking trays.

I like to use my blender to make the pizza dough. Add the yoghurt, flour, salt and oil to the blender and watch them come together and spin into a ball. Divide the dough into two equal portions, then, working with one portion at a time, knead the dough into two soft balls. Wrap them in plastic wrap and whack them in the fridge for 10 minutes.

Take the dough balls out of the fridge and flatten them on a lightly floured work surface the best way you can. I personally like to use a wine bottle because I get to drink the wine first; otherwise, use a rolling pin. Continue to flatten and roll the dough out into two 25–30 cm circles, then transfer them to your prepared trays.

Spread the tomato paste over the bases and top with the mozzarella, garlic and salami. Drizzle over the olive oil and sprinkle with the parmesan. Transfer to the oven and cook for 5–8 minutes, until the cheese is melted and bubbling.

Top the pizzas with the basil leaves, cut into slices and serve.

Bonus stuff

This recipe is all about the awesome pizza dough. The toppings are flexible and I encourage you to choose your own adventure. Cured meat is a favourite of mine because of the saltiness and oil it adds. I also love blue cheese, such as gorgonzola, and walnuts, but that's kind of gourmet and fancy pants.

'You'll high-five yourself after making this.'

CHEAT'S RICOTTA & FETA BUREK

Burek is my favourite Macedonian street food; it's the bomb. When I was five years old, my family took me to Macedonia and I tried burek for the first time. I was instantly sold and from that point on I was on a quest to find a burek to rival that first bite. Finally, after 40 years I found that bite in the Sydney suburb of Rockdale, from two inspiring brothers, Nikola and Jovan, aka the Burek Brothers. These guys generously shared their family recipe with me that dates back to 1926, and it inspired me to create my own cheat's version. Enjoy!

SERVES 4

Stuff you gotta get

3 tablespoons vegetable oil
375 g packet of frozen filo pastry, just thawed
250 g smooth ricotta
200 g feta

Now do this

You can cook the burek in an air fryer or the oven. If cooking in the oven, preheat it to 190°C. Grab a 30 cm round baking dish or something similar – you can even use a cake tin.

Using a pastry brush, lightly grease the dish with a little of the oil, then drop in two sheets of filo. Brush the pastry with oil and lay another two sheets on top. Spread half the ricotta all over the filo. The filo is fragile but don't stress if you tear it, it's all good. Crumble half the feta over the ricotta and add another two sheets of filo. Now stay with me for this next part: gently scrunch and bunch up parts of the filo to the give it some height. We want to create air pockets and fill the dish. Brush the top of the scrunched filo with a little more oil and top with another sheet, but leave it flat, tucking in the edges around the scrunched filo. Add the balance of the ricotta and feta, then add a final two sheets of filo to cover it all and brush generously with the balance of the vegetable oil.

Bake the burek in the oven for 25–30 minutes, until golden and crisp. If using an air fryer, cook at 180°C for 15 minutes. Slice it up and watch it disappear.

But wait, there's more!

Fillings are a matter of taste and preference. Burek is also often filled with mince and onion as well as ajvar (roasted red capsicum sauce), spinach or even pizza toppings.

You can easily convert this to a dessert burek: simply combine 2–3 grated apples, 3 tablespoons of brown sugar and a little ground cinnamon. You're very welcome.

My Cheat's Ricotta and Feta Burek is the bomb, whether it's for dinner or lunch the next day. Check out the previous page for the recipe (your kids will thank me!).

This Rustic Mediterranean Roulade (see page 61) is one of my favourite creations. It's basically your favourite antipasto ingredients all wrapped up in flaky puff pastry. Instant dinner and lunchbox classic!

MINI BEEF WELLINGTONS

Beef wellington is a Sunday-lunch favourite in our house. I love to get creative with the pastry, but you can also keep it simple. You don't even need to use beef, you can also use chicken, pork or even cauliflower. The first time I made this I almost killed my kids because I used spicy mustard, so make sure you pick a mustard that works for your little peeps. Okay, enough banter, let's do this.

SERVES 4

Grab all of this

40 g salted butter
4 x 200 g porterhouse steaks
2 teaspoons salt flakes
1 teaspoon freshly ground black pepper
4 sheets of frozen puff pastry, just thawed
1 tablespoon mustard of your choice
microwave vegetable gravy, to serve (optional)
your favourite veggie sides, to serve

Now the easy bit

Crank the oven to 180°C.

Melt the butter in a frying pan over medium–high heat. Add the steaks, laying them away from you to avoid splashing butter over yourself. Season with half the salt and pepper and sear for 90 seconds, then flip the steaks over, season with the remaining salt and pepper and sear for another 90 seconds. Transfer to a plate lined with paper towel to rest.

Lay the puff pastry sheets on a work surface and place a steak on one side of each pastry sheet. Smother the steaks with the mustard, then fold the pastry over the steaks and press down to seal. Trim the excess pastry around the edge of each pie and use it to make fancy decorations for the top of your pies. Or don't. It's up to you. You can also score a criss-cross pattern into the pastry as I have done here. Brush the butter left in the pan over the pastry, then transfer to a baking dish and whack them in the oven for 15 minutes.

Whip up a quick microwave vegetable gravy if you like. Serve alongside the beef wellingtons with your favourite veggie sides.

More stuff

You can use any protein or your favourite veg in this dish. This recipe is all about the pastry and how fancy you can make it to impress your family and little people. If you're not a fan of mustard, try coating the steaks in a smoky barbecue sauce instead.

SIMPLE BUTTER CHICKEN PIE

This dish really hits the spot. I love Indian food – the spices and aromas are to die for, but please don't die until you've tried this butter chicken pie. I thought I'd be clever by covering the chicken in pastry, which acts like the garlic naan we all love. When I make this, I often cook up some rice to serve on the side but it's also great on its own.

SERVES 4

Stuff you gotta get

40 g salted butter

1 onion, diced

3 garlic cloves, finely chopped

2 skinless and boneless chicken breasts, diced

150 g butter chicken curry paste

3 tablespoons tomato paste

400 ml can coconut cream

2 tablespoons plain flour

125 ml (½ cup) iced water

1 sheet of frozen puff pastry, just thawed

250 g packet of microwave basmati rice, to serve (optional)

coriander leaves, to serve (optional)

PASTRY GLAZE

2 garlic cloves

40 g salted butter

Let's rock

Preheat the oven to 180°C. Grease a 25 cm round baking dish.

Drop the butter, onion, garlic and chicken into a frying pan over medium heat. Cook, stirring, for 3–4 minutes, until the chicken is lightly seared, then add the butter chicken curry paste and tomato paste and stir through. Pour in the coconut cream and let it simmer for a couple of minutes.

Mix the flour and iced water in a small bowl to create a smooth slurry, then stir it through the chicken mixture and let it simmer for 5 minutes or until thickened.

Meanwhile, to make the pastry glaze, grate the garlic into a ramekin and add the butter. Zap it in the microwave on high in 10 second bursts until the butter has melted.

Transfer the butter chicken to the baking dish, lay the puff pastry sheet on top and trim the edges to fit (you can use the offcuts to make a pattern on top if you like). Brush the pastry with some of the melted garlic butter.

Bake the pie for 15 minutes or until golden brown. Glaze the pastry with the remaining garlic butter and let it rest for a couple of minutes. This is all the time you need to microwave the rice according to the packet instructions, if using.

Transfer the rice to a serving bowl and scatter the coriander leaves on top if desired. To serve, stick a large spoon in the pie and watch your family fight for it.

Did you know?

You can also use Thai curry paste to make this pie, but remember to check the spice level of the paste first. Simply add your favourite Thai-style veg, such as spring onion and carrot, along with the chicken. The secret is to thicken the sauce to make it pie-like.

RUSTIC MEDITERRANEAN ROULADE

When I think of Mediterranean food I think of antipasti, such as olives, feta, sundried tomatoes and cured meats, and fresh salads with balsamic vinegar. I thought there had to be a way to combine all of these delicious ingredients into a dinner that my family would love. So I created this rustic roulade that's easy to make, quick to cook and delicious to eat.

SERVES 4

What you'll need

3 sheets of frozen puff pastry, just thawed

200 g feta, crumbled

200 g pitted black olives, roughly chopped

200 g sundried tomatoes, roughly chopped

100 g sliced prosciutto, torn

100 g sliced Italian salami

120 g baby spinach leaves

½ eggplant, sliced into thin rounds

small bunch of asparagus, woody ends trimmed, roughly chopped

2 tablespoons balsamic glaze (see Handy Hints on page 32)

1 egg, lightly beaten

leafy salad, to serve

Now what?

Preheat the oven to 180°C. Line a baking tray with baking paper.

Now, lay your sheets of pastry side by side with a 2–3 cm overlap. Gently press down where the pastry sheets meet so they're stuck together and you will have one large rectangle.

Scatter the feta, olives, sundried tomato, prosciutto, salami, spinach, eggplant and asparagus over the pastry in an even layer, leaving a 2 cm border on all sides. Drizzle the balsamic glaze over the top, then, starting at a short end, gently roll up the pastry into a roulade. If any of the ingredients fall out, simply eat them (although maybe not the raw eggplant).

Brush the pastry with the beaten egg and whack it in the oven for 20 minutes or until the pastry is golden and cooked through.

Slice it up and serve with a delicious leafy salad.

Extra awesome stuff

You can chop and change any of the ingredients to create your own roulade – there are no hard and fast rules here. It's about discovering the foods you love and incorporating them into my recipes.

You can easily make this a vegetarian delight. Simply swap out the meats for your favourite veggies.

PIZZA SCROLL BAKE
(FOR FUSSY LITTLE HUMANS)

There was zero chance of me not including a pizza scroll recipe in this book. This is a cool way to make pizza for dinner without the hassle of making pizza dough. I use four different fillings in this recipe, so there'll be something for everyone, even the fussiest eaters. Using puff pastry makes this cost effective and awesome for school lunches the next day, if there's any left.

SERVES 4

Grab all of this

8 sheets of frozen puff pastry, just thawed
250 ml (1 cup) pizza sauce
150 g (1 cup) grated mozzarella, plus extra for sprinkling
salad of your choice, to serve

HAM AND PINEAPPLE

150 g (½ cup) shredded ham
¼ cup crushed canned pineapple

DIAVOLO

16 slices of salami
3 tablespoons chopped basil leaves

VEGGIE

45 g (½ cup) sliced mushrooms
60 g (½ cup) pitted black olives

Let's rock

Preheat the oven to 180°C. Grab a pizza tray or shallow, round baking dish and grease it or line with baking paper.

Cut each pastry sheet into four even-sized strips. Smear the pizza sauce onto the strips and top with the mozzarella. Set aside eight strips as these will be margarita pizza scrolls. Now top eight strips with the ham and pineapple, another eight with the diavolo toppings and the final eight with the veggie toppings.

Working with one strip at a time, fold the pastry strips in half lengthways to enclose the fillings, then roll them up into scrolls. Transfer the scrolls to the prepared pizza tray or dish and sprinkle with some extra mozzarella.

Transfer to the oven and bake for 18–20 minutes, until puffed up and golden. Allow to cool slightly, then allow everyone to choose their own pizza scrolls. Serve with a salad of your choice.

Handy hints

Pizza toppings are all a matter of choice, so pick your favourites and have fun. I would never put pineapple on a pizza, but I have little peeps who enjoy it so it's irrelevant what I think. This is also a cool recipe to get everyone involved in the kitchen as it's super easy to make.

BALKAN MINCE PIE

This Balkan mince pie is similar to the famous Aussie meat pie, but instead it's made with filo pastry and the filling options are huge. I used to eat it all the time when I was a kid – Mum would put it in my school lunchbox at least once a week and I clearly remember my Aussie mates wondering what on earth I was eating. My mum would make it with a cheese filling, but in recent years I've been rocking the meat version instead.

SERVES 4

What you'll need

1 tablespoon olive oil
1 onion, finely chopped
500 g pork and veal mince
1 tablespoon salt flakes
1 teaspoon freshly ground
  black pepper
1 tablespoon smoked paprika
10 sheets of filo pastry
vegetable oil, for brushing
1 egg, lightly beaten
1 tablespoon sesame seeds
garden salad, to serve

Rock it like this

Preheat the oven to 180°C. Grease a pizza tray with oil.

Heat the olive oil in a large frying pan over medium heat. Add the onion and cook for 2–3 minutes to sweat it out a little, then add the mince and cook, breaking up any lumps with the back of a wooden spoon, for 5 minutes, until starting to brown. Add the salt, pepper and smoked paprika and stir through. Continue to cook for 3 minutes or until the mince is cooked through, then remove the pan from the heat. You can cook the mince the night before and keep it in the fridge, if you prefer.

Take out your first sheet of filo pastry and lay it flat on a clean work surface in front of you. Lightly dip a pastry brush into the vegetable oil and brush it over the filo sheet. Spoon 2 tablespoons of the mince mixture in a long horizontal strip, 3 cm in from the edge of the pastry closest to you. Fold the edge of the pastry over the filling and keep rolling all the way to the end until you have a sausage. Now roll it like a scroll, in on itself, and pop it in the middle of the pizza tray. Continue this process using the remaining mince mixture and pastry, and wrapping around the previous scroll until you have a large circular pie.

Once your filo circle is complete, brush the top with the beaten egg and sprinkle with the sesame seeds. Bake for 20 minutes or until the pastry is golden brown. Serve with a fresh garden salad.

More stuff

To make a cheese version of this pie, combine 1 cup each of creamy ricotta and feta. The sky is the limit with fillings, so don't hold back.

I like to crumble feta into my garden salad for an extra salty, tangy hit. Try it! You won't be disappointed.

'This pie rocks, almost as much as my mum.'

I couldn't write a book without including a recipe for pizza scrolls. My Pizza Scroll Bake (see page 62) has four different options for fillings so your kids can pick and choose their favourites. Perfect lunchbox size, too.

Introducing my Balkan Mince Pie – similar to an Aussie meat pie, only better! Flip back a page for the recipe. I bet it's going to become a firm favourite.

Fast and fresh meals for when you are having an 'I can't be stuffed making dinner' moment

PASTA, NOODLES & RICE

15-MINUTE CHEESE & BACON PASTA

I love the versatility of this recipe as you can use the sauce as a base to make other simple pasta dishes, such as mac 'n' cheese and carbonara. Even though it only takes 15 minutes to make from start to finish, it looks like a lot of effort has gone into it. I sometimes make this with spaghetti, but I've decided to use penne here. Is there anything better than cheese and bacon pasta?

SERVES 4

Stuff you gotta get

500 g dried penne
250 ml (1 cup) full-cream milk
250 g (2 cups) grated cheddar
60 g salted butter, diced
250 g bacon, diced
2 tablespoons grated parmesan
½ cup finely chopped flat-leaf parsley leaves
crusty bread, to serve
Italian salad (see More Stuff on page 42), to serve

Now do this

Bring a large saucepan of salted water to the boil over high heat. Add the penne and cook according to the packet instructions, until al dente.

While the pasta is cooking, heat the milk in a saucepan over medium heat. Allow the milk to come to a simmer, then add half the grated cheddar, one handful at a time. Add the butter and stir until melted, then add the remaining cheddar, one handful at a time, followed by the bacon and parmesan for that extra flavour bang.

Drain the pasta, but try to leave about 125 ml (½ cup) of water in the pan. Return the pasta to the pan, place over low heat and stir through the cheese sauce, making sure the pasta is well coated in all the creamy goodness. Transfer the pasta to a large serving bowl and sprinkle the parsley over the top.

I like to serve this in the middle of the table with crusty bread and an Italian salad. Invite everyone to help themselves – I love watching my kids dip the bread in the sauce.

Did you know?

You can use chicken instead of bacon, but make sure it's cooked before adding it to the cheese sauce.

You can also swap out the cheddar for another good melting cheese of your choice.

'Just make a heap of noise in the kitchen and everyone will think you're busy.'

MIDWEEK CHICKEN PASTA BAKE

This is the perfect 'I can't be stuffed making dinner' recipe. We all have those moments during the week when we can't be bothered, but we still have to make a good feed for the family. This chicken pasta bake ticks all those boxes. I love how it seems like a lot of effort has gone into it, when, in fact, you can put it together in minutes.

SERVES 4

Grab all of this

500 g dried penne
2 tablespoons olive oil
1 kg skinless chicken thigh fillets
1 tablespoon salt flakes
1 tablespoon garlic powder
300 ml thickened cream
2 tablespoons grated parmesan
1 tablespoon Vegeta stock powder
125 g (1 cup) grated cheddar
leafy salad, to serve

Now what?

Preheat the oven to 180°C.

Bring a large saucepan of salted water to the boil and cook the penne according to the packet instructions, until al dente.

While the pasta is cooking, heat the olive oil in a large frying pan over high heat. Season the chicken with the salt and garlic powder and sear for 5 minutes each side until golden brown (we don't want to cook the chicken through, as it will finish cooking in the oven). Grab a baking dish and line up the chicken thighs in a single layer in the dish.

Drain the penne and return it the saucepan. Stir in the cream, parmesan and Vegeta stock powder until the pasta is completely coated in the creamy goodness, then pour it around the chicken in the baking dish. Sprinkle the cheddar all over the pasta, avoiding the chicken, then transfer to the oven and bake for 15 minutes or until the cheese is beautifully melted and the chicken is cooked through.

Invite everyone to the table and serve with a leafy salad.

Extra awesome stuff

If you like a bit of punch in your meals, stir through ¼ cup of crumbled blue cheese and a few crushed garlic cloves with the cream and parmesan. If you want to cheat your way through this meal even more, you can use a supermarket whole roast chicken. Simply shred the chicken instead of cooking up the thigh fillets.

ONE-PAN RICE & VEGGIES

Ridiculously FAST!

Just throw everything in the pan and all will be okay. This recipe is literally that easy. It's inspired by risotto, but I like to think of it as more edgy and with more punch. I use different vegetables every time I make this, as it's a great way to use up what's left in the crisper drawer before the next trip to the supermarket.

SERVES 4

What you'll need

1 tablespoon olive oil
1 onion, diced
3 garlic cloves, crushed
4 small chorizo sausages, diced
2 carrots, diced
1 zucchini, sliced into half moons
1 teaspoon salt flakes
1 teaspoon smoked paprika
10 cherry tomatoes, halved
2 x 250 g packets of microwave
  long-grain white or brown rice
200 ml vegetable stock
1 red capsicum, sliced into strips
1 green capsicum, sliced into strips
leafy salad, to serve

Let's rock

Heat the olive oil in a large saucepan over medium heat. Add the onion, garlic and chorizo and cook for 3–4 minutes, until the chorizo is lightly browned. Add the carrot, zucchini, salt, paprika and cherry tomatoes and stir it all together.

Meanwhile, microwave the rice according to the packet instructions. Add the rice to the pan, along with the vegetable stock and simmer, stirring every now and then, for 5 minutes. Stir through the red and green capsicum and cook for another 5 minutes.

At this stage the smell in your kitchen should be next level. You'll be feeling really hungry, so it's time to have a taste test and check for seasoning.

Divide the rice and veggies among plates and serve with your favourite leafy salad.

More stuff

As well as being similar to risotto, I also think this dish has a slight paella feel to it. The idea is that the veggies and rice absorb the flavour of the spices and smoky chorizo.

Feel free to add any veggies that you might have left in your fridge, or use other sausages that you know your family will love.

For something a little different in your lunchbox, try my Speedy Lamb Salad (see page 38). It's delicious either on its own or served over some white rice.

PORK, FENNEL & TOMATO PASTA

When you take your first bite of this dish you'll be immediately transported to a traditional restaurant in Southern Italy! My big sister Suzy makes this dish really well, and she often mixes up the sausages to create different flavours.

SERVES 4

Grab the following

2 tablespoons olive oil

1 onion, diced

4 garlic cloves, finely chopped

4 pork and fennel sausages

400 g can whole peeled tomatoes

250 ml (1 cup) white wine

1 teaspoon salt flakes

1 teaspoon freshly ground
  black pepper

500 g fresh egg pasta, such as
  tagliatelle

½ cup basil leaves

grated parmesan, to serve

Let's rock

Heat the olive oil in a large frying pan over medium heat. Add the onion and garlic and cook for 3–4 minutes, until soft and translucent. Chop one end off each sausage and simply squeeze the meat into the pan, breaking it up with a wooden spoon. Stir through the tomatoes, then add the white wine and take a step back while the alcohol cooks out. You'll know this is done when you can no longer smell the wine! Season with the salt and pepper.

Meanwhile, bring a large saucepan of salted water to the boil and cook the pasta according to the packet instructions, until al dente. Drain the pasta, reserving 125 ml (½ cup) of the cooking water.

Easy so far? We are almost done. Add the reserved pasta cooking water to the sauce and simmer for 15 minutes or until the sauce is reduced and slightly thickened. Add the pasta to the pan and flip it (or maybe don't) and stir through the sauce until the pasta is completely coated. Add the basil leaves at the last minute – we want them to remain as fresh as possible.

Divide among serving bowls, top with a little grated parmesan and serve immediately.

Did you know?

You can use your favourite sausages to change up the overall flavour, but I personally think that the pork and fennel really make this dish. Back in the day someone must have gone to a lot of effort to invent that flavour profile, so I like to take advantage of it!

SPECIAL FRIED RICE WITH PRAWNS

Who doesn't love a good fried rice? When I buy fresh prawns from the deli
I sometimes choose ones that are already marinated to save me the hassle of doing
it myself. It's also a good opportunity to try new flavours and combinations.
Sometimes the easiest recipes are the best. Exhibit A!

SERVES 6

Grab the following

- 2 x 450 g packets of microwave long-grain white rice
- 70 g (1 cup) broccoli florets
- 125 g (1 cup) cauliflower florets
- 2 tablespoons sesame oil
- 1 tablespoon grated garlic
- 1 tablespoon grated ginger
- 1 kg peeled raw prawns
- 100 g (1 cup) sugar snap peas, trimmed
- 1 tablespoon fish sauce
- 3 tablespoons soy sauce
- 1 spring onion, finely sliced on an angle
- ¼ cup coriander leaves
- 2 tablespoons fried shallots

Let's rock it like this

Put your kettle on to boil. Whack the rice in the microwave and cook according to the packet instructions.

Place the broccoli and cauliflower in a heatproof bowl, pour over enough boiling water to cover and leave to blanch for about 2 minutes. Drain well.

If you have a wok, you rock! Alternatively, use a large frying pan. Heat the sesame oil in the wok or pan over high heat. Add the garlic, ginger and prawns and stir-fry for 2–3 minutes, then add the drained broccoli and cauliflower and sugar snap peas and stir-fry for 1 minute. Add the cooked rice, fish sauce and soy sauce and stir-fry for 1 minute, until the rice has turned a light brown from the soy sauce.

Divide the fried rice among serving bowls and top with the spring onion, coriander leaves and fried shallots.

Handy hints

You can easily swap out the prawns for chicken, beef, pork or tofu, or change the veggies to whatever you have in the crisper drawer. The key ingredients to this special fried rice are the ginger, garlic, fish sauce and soy sauce. If you keep these ingredients, you're destined to achieve greatness.

Try my zingy Vietnamese Noodle Salad (see page 157) for something a little different for lunch. Top it with slices of roasted chicken for a protein boost.

READY-IN-A-FLASH VEGGIE & NOODLE STIR-FRY

Ridiculously
FAST!

This is the ultimate clean-out-the-fridge veggie stir-fry. What I love about stir-fries is that you can use almost any combination of vegetables, then simply add a few classic Asian flavours to make those veggies sing. Let's make this happen!

SERVES 4

What you'll need

- **3 x 90 g packets of 2-minute noodles**
- **2 tablespoons vegetable or sesame oil**
- **1 onion, chopped**
- **1 tablespoon ginger paste**
- **1 tablespoon crushed garlic**
- **70 g (1 cup) broccoli florets**
- **125 g (1 cup) cauliflower florets**
- **2 tablespoons fish sauce**
- **3 tablespoons soy sauce**
- **100 g (1 cup) sugar snap peas, trimmed**
- **½ red capsicum, sliced**
- **½ green capsicum, sliced**
- **90 g (1 cup) bean sprouts**
- **½ cup chopped coriander leaves**
- **80 g (½ cup) crushed peanuts**

Now the easy bit

Prepping the ingredients is the hardest part of this recipe, so it's easy from here on in. Cook the noodles according to the packet instructions, then drain and set aside.

Heat the oil in a wok or large frying pan over high heat. Add the onion, ginger paste and garlic and stir-fry for about 30 seconds, then add the broccoli and cauliflower and cook for 1–2 minutes. Add the fish sauce and soy sauce, then drop in the noodles and stir well. Add the sugar snap peas and capsicums, flipping the wok if you're at expert level, otherwise stirring like crazy so the ingredients don't stick to the base of the pan. Cook for about 2 minutes, until the vegetables are just cooked through but still a little crisp.

Transfer the stir-fry to a large serving dish or individual bowls, top with the bean sprouts, coriander leaves and crushed peanuts and don't forget the chopsticks.

But wait, there's more!

You can easily add any protein to this recipe to make it a beef, pork or chicken stir-fry; heck, you could even add tofu, too. But let's not get carried away. Lol. If you do add a protein, make sure you cook it off first and reduce the amount of veggies.

SALMON & AVO SUSHI BOWL

Ridiculously FAST!

A good sushi roll is all about using quality ingredients, such as avocado and salmon, and having an awesome sauce. It's almost too good to keep wrapped up. That's why I invented this recipe: why hide delicious ingredients in a roll when you can showcase them in a bowl for your family to really appreciate. The best thing about this dish is just how easy it is to assemble as you don't have to cook anything. Win–win!

SERVES 4

What you'll need

2 x 250 g packets of microwave long-grain white rice

2 tablespoons rice wine vinegar

1 tablespoon sesame oil

2 teaspoons caster sugar

1 cup shredded iceberg lettuce

1 carrot, julienned

1 avocado, sliced

2 teaspoons poppy seeds

500 g smoked salmon

1 Lebanese cucumber, julienned

2 spring onions, finely sliced on an angle

2 teaspoons sesame seeds

4 sheets of yaki nori seaweed, torn (optional)

CREAMY WASABI DRESSING

125 g (½ cup) mayonnaise

1 teaspoon wasabi paste

1 teaspoon sesame oil

½ teaspoon salt flakes

Now do this

Pop the rice in the microwave and cook according to the packet instructions. Transfer to a large bowl, add the rice wine vinegar, sesame oil and sugar and give it a good mix. Set aside.

Let's make the creamy wasabi dressing next. Place all the ingredients in a small bowl and mix until well combined. Set aside.

Divide the rice among four deep serving bowls, then it is time to assemble! I like to place the lettuce and carrot next to each other for colour contrast. Now position the avocado next to the carrot and sprinkle the poppy seeds over top. Add the smoked salmon, cucumber and spring onion in their own separate piles and scatter over the sesame seeds. You can pour the creamy wasabi dressing over the whole lot or serve it in a small bowl alongside for dipping into. Finally, add the yaki nori (if using) to each bowl – my youngest, Kiki, loves it whereas Anela isn't a fan. Alternatively, you can place all the ingredients in separate bowls and let everyone assemble their own sushi bowls at the table. Find a few chopsticks and serve.

Extra awesome stuff

This is a great way to introduce your little peeps to fresh and healthy food. Sushi bowls are full of good carbs, healthy fats, lean protein and fresh veggies; it seriously doesn't get better than that.

The sky's the limit when choosing different proteins to add to your sushi bowl. I once made it with tempura chicken, which totally rocked with the creamy wasabi dressing. You can also chop and change the vegetables to whatever you have in the fridge.

Feel free to increase the amount of wasabi in the dressing, or omit it completely if you're not a fan of heat.

BAKED RISOTTO WITH PANCETTA & SUGAR SNAPS

Chuck it in, it'll be right! This is the attitude I take whenever I make this risotto. I've tweaked the recipe a few times since first eating it at my sister Suzy's place many, many years ago. The pancetta is the secret: the smell and crispness is next level and I highly recommend you add a few extra slices for yourself while no one else is looking. Let's get crackling, I mean cracking.

SERVES 4

Grab all of this

2 tablespoons vegetable oil
1 onion, chopped
4 garlic cloves, finely sliced
440 g (2 cups) arborio rice
1 litre (4 cups) vegetable stock
1 tablespoon Vegeta stock powder
300 g sliced pancetta
100 g (1 cup) sugar snap peas, trimmed
50 g salted butter
75 g (¾ cup) grated parmesan
1 tablespoon extra-virgin olive oil
60 g baby rocket

It's time to do this

Preheat the oven to 180°C. Line a baking tray with baking paper.

Heat the vegetable oil in a flameproof casserole dish over medium heat. Add the onion and garlic and cook for 2–3 minutes, until soft and translucent. Add the rice and give it a good stir for about 1 minute, then add 250 ml (1 cup) of the vegetable stock and let it simmer until the stock has almost disappeared. Pour in the remaining vegetable stock and the Vegeta, then cover with the lid or foil and pop it in the oven for 30 minutes.

Meanwhile, place the pancetta on the prepared tray and bake in the oven for the last 15 minutes of the risotto cooking time, until crisp. Keep an eye on it as the thickness of the slices will determine just how quickly they cook.

Now blanch the sugar snap peas in boiling water for 1–2 minutes, then drain and set aside.

Remove the risotto from the oven and stir through the butter, parmesan, olive oil, sugar snap peas and half the rocket. Scatter the remaining rocket over the risotto and position the pancetta on top (making sure you eat a few slices while no one is looking). Divide among shallow bowls and serve.

Did you know?

If you're vegetarian, replace the pancetta with finely sliced tofu sprinkled with smoked paprika and salt. Cook for the same amount of time and scatter over the top before serving. You could also use 'facon' (fake bacon) instead, along with vegan cheese and butter to make the risotto entirely vegan.

Some people say that you need to add dry white wine before the stock for it to be a real risotto, but my little peeps simply don't like the taste, so I exclude it and add the Vegeta stock powder instead.

Cracking fish and seafood dinners that will have the whole family hooked

SUPER-FAST SEAFOOD

VERMICELLI-WRAPPED PRAWNS WITH SWEET CHILLI SAUCE

Prawns are so awesome and delicious, plus they're full of vitamins. This recipe was inspired by a meal my wife and I had at the restaurant I proposed to her in: Trilogy at the Park Hyatt in Melbourne. I have no idea how they made their dish, but my version is fast, simple and delicious. I love that seafood cooks quickly, which means you can whip this up in no time.

SERVES 4

What you'll need

150 g vermicelli rice noodles

500 g large peeled raw prawns (tails on or off, whichever you prefer)

1 tablespoon sesame oil

½ teaspoon salt flakes

½ teaspoon freshly ground black pepper

500 ml (2 cups) vegetable oil

2 x 250 g packets of microwave long-grain white rice

125 ml (½ cup) sweet chilli sauce

1 long red chilli, sliced (optional)

Let's rock

Place the noodles in a bowl, cover with water and let them soak for about 15 minutes, until soft.

Rinse the prawns and pat them dry with paper towel to remove excess moisture; otherwise they'll spit when they hit the hot oil.

Don't be afraid to get your hands dirty for this next part. Drain the noodles and place them in a bowl, then pour the sesame oil over the noodles and add the salt and pepper. Mix it all together with your hands to make sure the noodles have a nice, even coverage.

Heat the vegetable oil in a wok or deep frying pan over medium heat. The oil is ready when you drop a vermicelli noodle into it and it puffs up immediately.

While the oil is heating, grab a small handful of noodles and start wrapping the prawns individually – I like to go heavy on the noodles and double wrap the prawns. I just love the crunch they create and I assure you that your little humans will love them, too.

Working in batches, carefully lower the wrapped prawns into the hot oil and watch the magic happen. As soon as the vermicelli noodles puff up and turn golden brown, use a slotted spoon to remove the prawns and pop them on paper towel to drain.

Microwave the rice according to the packet instructions, then transfer to serving bowls. Top with the prawns, drizzle over the sweet chilli sauce and scatter with slices of red chilli, if you like.

Extra awesome stuff

For a summery twist, ditch the sweet chilli sauce and serve with a mango salad. Simply dice a couple of mangos and combine with julienned carrot and cucumber, shredded baby cos lettuce, a little finely chopped red chilli and my Vietnamese dressing on page 31.

The secret to this dish is to rock the crunch, so don't be afraid to overload the prawns with the vermicelli noodles.

'It doesn't get Eddie Vedder than this.'

NO-FUSS BAKED SALMON WITH POTATOES & VEG

There's something special about oven bakes, they feel almost too easy because you're technically just throwing everything into a dish and the oven does the rest. So when you try this recipe, do what I do and pretend to make a fuss. Let everyone know you're cooking by talking out loud to yourself. Say, 'where's the baking dish?', or, 'if only someone else cooked for once', and my personal favourite, 'everyone would starve if I died'. So grab your baking dish and let's start the salmon party.

SERVES 4

Grab this stuff

400 g packet of microwave baby potatoes
400 g packet of microwave mixed veggies
3 tablespoons olive oil
4 garlic cloves
6 x 150 g skin-on salmon fillets
80 g salted butter
1 teaspoon salt flakes
1 teaspoon freshly ground black pepper

It's time to do this

Preheat the oven to 200°C.

Microwave your potatoes and veggies according to the packet instructions, but only cook the veggies for half the time it recommends. Got it?

Pour the olive oil into a large baking dish, making sure the base is completely coated. Once the potatoes and veggies are ready, tip them into the baking dish.

Finely grate the garlic into a small ramekin.

Pop the salmon in the baking dish amongst the veggies, skin-side down, and smear the garlic on top. Melt the butter in the microwave by zapping it on high in 10-second bursts. Pour the melted butter over the salmon, potatoes and veggies and remember to season everything with the salt and pepper.

Cover the dish with foil and bake for 5 minutes, then remove the foil, reduce the heat to 180°C and cook for another 5 minutes.

When you serve the salmon, make sure you spoon the buttery sauce over the top. The smell of garlic will get the appetite going in no time.

More stuff

You can also roast the potatoes with your favourite veggies. This is simply my time-poor version. We all know that potatoes take ages in the oven so the microwave packet option is a real winner.

QUICK THAI GREEN CURRY WITH BARRAMUNDI

I'm not sure if I can say this in a book, but this sh*t is the bomb! As far as flavour explosions go it doesn't get better than this, plus it's so easy to make. When I did a cooking course in Thailand many years ago, my mind was blown at how many ingredients went into the green curry paste. There was no way I was going to make it at home as it was so time-consuming. Fast forward a few years and many grey hairs later, you can thankfully now buy Thai green curry paste in a jar at the supermarket. My problem was over!

SERVES 4

Grab the following

1 tablespoon vegetable oil
3 garlic cloves, crushed
100 g Thai green curry paste
150 g (1½ cups) sugar snap peas
400 ml can coconut cream
4 x 200–250 g skinless boneless barramundi fillets, at room temperature
2 x 250 g packets of microwave jasmine rice
⅓ cup coriander leaves
45 g (½ cup) bean sprouts
3 tablespoons crushed peanuts
1 long red chilli, finely sliced

Now the easy bit

Fire up the wok or a large frying pan over medium heat, pour in the vegetable oil and let it heat up. Add the garlic and Thai green curry paste and stir for 3–4 minutes, until the spice hits your eyes and you want to cry.

Meanwhile, prepare the sugar snap peas. Working with one sugar snap pea at a time, pinch off one end and gently pull to remove the fibrous spine. This is the bit that gets stuck in your teeth and no one wants that!

Add the sugar snap peas and coconut cream to the wok or frying pan and bring to a simmer. Add the fish – I use my fingers to break it up into bite-sized chunks as I add it to the pan – and simmer, stirring occasionally, for about 6 minutes, until the fish is cooked through. See how easy that was?

Finally, microwave the rice according to the packet instructions.

To serve, I think a large shallow serving bowl showcases this dish best. You can serve the rice on the side or underneath the curry, or even fill a cup with rice and flip it onto plates to get that corny Thai takeaway restaurant vibe, which is also pretty cool. Top the curry with the coriander, bean sprouts, crushed peanuts and chilli.

Regardless of how you serve this dish, it's tasty as, so enjoy and peace out, homies.

Handy hints

If you want to mix it up, try swapping the fish for chicken, beef strips or even prawns – the sky's the limit! You can also make a vegan version using tofu and heaps of vegetables.

These days, most supermarkets also stock red curry and satay pastes, so be adventurous and try them all out.

GRILLED TUNA STEAKS WITH POTATO SALAD

Cooking fish on a weeknight is awesome. I can have dinner on the table in less than 20 minutes, leaving me with more time to do what I need to do, like rest. Tuna is full of nutrients and vitamins, and if you're in training mode this recipe will rock your workout world. Kiki, my youngest, absolutely loves tuna – she likes it seared and pink on the inside, which is exactly how I like it, too. However, I have to overcook it for Anela and my wife. Even though tuna is quite expensive, this dish is still cheaper than fast-food takeaway.

SERVES 4

Grab all of this

400 g packet of microwave baby potatoes
2 tablespoons olive oil
250 g mixed medley cherry tomatoes, halved
4 x 250 g tuna steaks
1 teaspoon salt flakes
1 teaspoon freshly ground black pepper
⅓ cup chopped basil leaves
½ teaspoon finely grated lemon zest
juice of ½ lemon

Now do this

Fire up the barbecue grill or use a chargrill pan – we want to put some nice grill marks on the tuna steaks.

Meanwhile, whack the packet of baby potatoes in the microwave and cook according to the packet instructions. Pop them in a mixing bowl, add 1 tablespoon of the oil and stir through.

Pop the cherry tomatoes on the grill or in the pan and cook for about 3 minutes, until just starting to caramelise – we don't want to cook them all the way through, but just enough so that they become a little sweet. Transfer to a bowl and set aside.

Gently rub the remaining olive oil over the tuna steaks and season with the salt and ½ teaspoon of the pepper. Pop the tuna on the grill or in the pan and cook for about 2 minutes each side. Make sure you're happy with the grill marks on the tuna as that's the wow factor that is going to impress the harshest food critics (your little humans).

Remove the tuna from the grill, cover with foil and set aside to rest for a few minutes – it will continue to cook through while resting.

Add the basil, lemon zest, lemon juice and remaining pepper to the potatoes. Mix well, then divide among four plates.

Add the grilled tuna steaks to the plates, then top with the tomatoes. Enjoy!

Extra awesome stuff

This recipe has a Mediterranean vibe, but you could also try a honey, ginger and sesame glaze for the tuna and then serve it on a bed of rice for an Asian twist.

You can also use swordfish or another similar meaty fish. I usually avoid cooking white fish on the barbecue grill as it has a tendency to fall apart.

ANGELIC PRAWN PASTA

Prawns are easy to prepare and quick to cook, making them the ideal dinner for when you want to chill out and watch Netflix. These days, supermarket delis have some pretty awesome stuff on offer, including garlic-marinated prawns, which I use in this recipe. In Italy, they never add parmesan to seafood pasta dishes, so don't tell anyone if you sprinkle some on top!

SERVES 4

Grab the following

500 g dried angel hair pasta

2 tablespoons extra-virgin olive oil

1 kg marinated garlic prawns from the deli counter

150 g (1 cup) mixed medley cherry tomatoes, halved

1 tablespoon salt flakes

½ cup finely chopped flat-leaf parsley leaves

1 baguette, sliced, to serve (optional)

Time to get cracking

Bring a large saucepan of salted water to the boil over high heat. Add the angel hair pasta, but don't break the pasta in half as this is a big no-no in Italy. Cook the pasta according to the packet instructions, until al dente

While your pasta is cooking, grab a large frying pan, add the olive oil and place over medium heat. Drop in the garlic prawns and cherry tomatoes and cook, turning occasionally, for 3–4 minutes, until the prawns are pink and cooked through.

Using tongs, lift the cooked pasta from the boiling water and add it to the cooked prawns and tomatoes, along with 125 ml (½ cup) of the pasta cooking water. Sprinkle the salt over the top, add the parsley and toss together until warmed through.

Divide the pasta and prawns among bowls and serve with some sliced baguette, if you like.

But wait, there's more!

Angel hair pasta is a thin, noodle-like pasta, but you can use other varieties, too, such as spaghetti or tagliatelle.

You can add dried chilli flakes or sliced fresh chilli to the garlic prawns. The heat takes this dish to the next level, but remember your little humans might not like the spice.

Supermarket deli counters sometimes sell different varieties of marinated prawns, so don't be afraid to try them out.

LEMON-BAKED FISH WITH BUTTERY MASH

White fish is tender and easy to cook; it's also really good for you and we enjoy it at home at least once a week, served with my delicious buttery mash. The type of white fish isn't too important – just head to your local fishmonger or deli and grab the freshest fish available. Actually, don't grab it, let them do that.

SERVES 4

Ingredients you'll need

4 x 150–200 g skinless firm white fish fillets, such as butterfish
40 g salted butter, melted
1 teaspoon salt flakes
1 tablespoon snipped chives
1 lemon, finely sliced

BUTTERY MASH

1 kg red royale potatoes, peeled and chopped into bite-sized pieces
200 g salted butter, chopped, plus extra to serve
250 ml (1 cup) full-cream milk
1 tablespoon salt flakes

Let's rock

Preheat the oven to 180°C. Line a baking tray with baking paper.

To make the buttery mash, bring a large saucepan of salted water to the boil over high heat. Add the potato, reduce the heat to a rapid simmer and cover with the lid to speed up the cooking process. Cook for about 8 minutes, until tender.

While your spuds are cooking, brush the fish with the melted butter, sprinkle the salt and chives over the top, then lay the lemon slices, overlapping, on top of the fish. Pop the fish on the prepared tray, then transfer to the oven and cook for 15 minutes or until opaque and just cooked through (the cooking time may vary depending on the thickness of the fish).

Drain the potato and return it to the pan, along with the butter. Place over low heat and pour in the milk. Grab a potato masher and start mashing the potato – you'll need to go hard as we want the butter and milk to dissolve into the spuds. Add the salt and mix through, then taste test to make sure you're happy with the seasoning.

Serving time. I love to simply take the baking dish with the fish over to the table and serve the buttery mash in a large bowl next to it. Don't forget to add a teaspoon of butter to the top of the mash for an extra touch of buttery delight.

Did you know?

I once ate mashed potato in the South of France where the quantities of butter and potato were equal: 500 g of spuds and 500 g of the best French butter! It tasted amazing, but it wasn't very healthy, so I've used far less butter in this recipe.

You can use any white fish in this dish or even firmer fish, such as swordfish or salmon. The advantage of white fish is that it cooks quickly and tastes light, which balances the heavy mash really well. Enjoy!

CRISPY FISH WITH SWEET POTATO CHIPS

This dish is at the top of my list for insanely good weeknight dinners. The crispy fish is so versatile: I often serve it in burgers or tacos, or even as finger food. Cooking the sweet potato in an air fryer speeds things up even more.

SERVES 4

What you'll need

100 g (1 cup) dried breadcrumbs
½ teaspoon salt flakes
1 teaspoon garlic powder
¼ cup crushed corn chips
75 g (½ cup) plain flour
2 eggs
4 x 250 g skinless boneless white fish fillets, such as butterfish or red emperor
125 ml (½ cup) vegetable oil (optional)
leafy salad, to serve
lemon wedges, to serve

SWEET POTATO CHIPS

1 large sweet potato
olive oil spray
1 teaspoon salt flakes

Rock it like this

You can cook the sweet potato chips in the oven or an air fryer. If cooking in the oven, preheat it to 190°C.

The first question with your sweet potato chips is, to peel or not to peel? Don't peel! All the nutrients are in the skin so leave it alone. Grab a sharp knife and slice the sweet potato into your favourite chip shape. I like to cut long sweet potato chips with a fat part at one end that you can hold. Pop the chips on a baking tray, spray with olive oil spray and sprinkle over the salt flakes. Cook in the oven for 40 minutes or in an air fryer at 185°C for 15 minutes or until cooked through.

While your sweet potato chips are cooking, grab three mixing bowls. Combine the breadcrumbs, salt, garlic powder and corn chips in one bowl, place the flour in another bowl and crack the eggs into the third bowl and lightly beat.

Pat the fish dry with paper towel. Working with one piece of fish at a time, toss the fish in the flour, then dip into the beaten egg. Finally, coat in the breadcrumb mixture. Pop the fish in a baking dish.

To shallow-fry the fish, heat the oil in a large frying pan over medium heat. Add the fish and cook for 3 minutes each side or until golden brown and cooked through.

If you'd like to cook the fish in the oven, reduce the temperature to 180°C and bake the fish for 12 minutes. If using an air fryer, cook at 170°C for 7 minutes.

Serve the fish with the sweet potato chips and a fresh leafy salad, with lemon wedges on the side for that citrus bang.

Bonus stuff

Feel free to swap the fish for chicken or any meat that your family love. Tofu also works really well.

Use regular potatoes instead of sweet potatoes to create the ultimate fish and chips.

EASY CHEESY FISH PIE

A simple fish pie that will earn you legend status in the kitchen is well worth making. I have made so many variations of this pie and they've all been pretty awesome, but this one is my favourite: it's super cheesy and super delicious. You can make this in either a baking dish or a cast-iron frying pan – whatever you've got in your kitchen.

SERVES 4

Stuff you gotta get

1 kg skinless barramundi fillets (or other firm white fish fillets)
100 g salted butter
3 shallots, sliced
2 garlic cloves, crushed
125 g (1 cup) grated cheddar
6 sheets of filo pastry
green leafy salad, to serve

Okay, let's get to it

Preheat the oven to 180°C.

Put the kettle on to boil and place the fish in a deep bowl or a saucepan. Pour the boiling water over the fish, making sure it is covered – it will turn white as it slowly poaches. Leave for about 5 minutes.

In the meantime, melt 80 g of the butter in a large, ovenproof cast-iron frying pan over medium heat. (The idea is that we start cooking this on the stovetop then transfer the pan to the oven. If you don't have an ovenproof frying pan, just use a regular one and we'll transfer to a baking dish later.) Once the butter starts to sizzle, drop in the shallot and garlic. Lean forward and inhale the aroma, it will hit the soul and heighten your hunger.

Gently drain the fish and transfer to a clean bowl. Use a fork to lightly break up the fish fillets, then add to the pan with the shallot and garlic. Turn off the heat and sprinkle over the cheese – it will slowly start to melt. If your frying pan isn't ovenproof, now is the time to transfer the fish mixture to a baking dish.

Grab your filo pastry and cover the cheesy fish. Give the pastry a little scrunch here and there to create some texture, and tuck the corners in around the filling.

Melt the remaining butter in the microwave and drizzle it over the pastry. Transfer the pan or dish to the oven and bake for 12–15 minutes, until the pastry is golden.

Serve the fish pie in the pan or dish with a big spoon for scooping out the deliciousness and a fresh leafy salad on the side.

More stuff

You can use any white fish to make this fish pie, just make sure that it's boneless. Also, remove the skin if it's still attached as we want the fish to melt in your mouth.

Ten clever ways to transform a supermarket roast chook into an awesome dinner

PIMP UP YOUR YOUR ROAST CHICKEN!

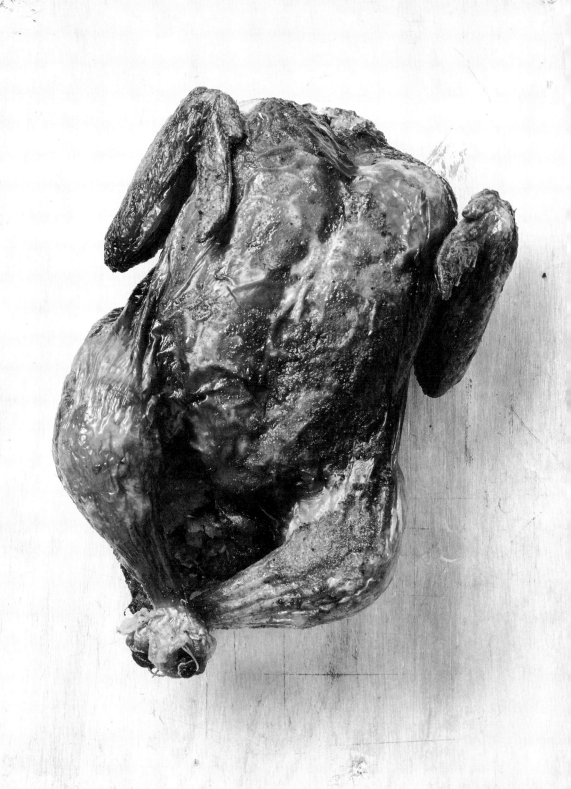

HOW TO DIVIDE
A WHOLE CHICKEN

When I was a kid I worked in a chicken shop and I mastered how to cut a whole chicken: the secret is to use kitchen scissors. It is so much easier to divide a chicken using a good, sharp pair of kitchen scissors than with a knife. Follow the steps below to divide a whole chicken neatly into either four or eight pieces.

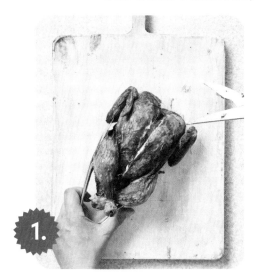

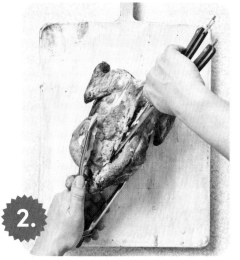

Place the chicken on a chopping board, breast-side up, and cut the breast in half along the breast bone.

Flip the chicken over and cut along one side of the back bone, then the other. Remove and discard the back bone.

Next, cut the drumstick and thigh from the breast and wing to create four roughly equal portions.

Use as is, or to divide into eight portions, simply cut the drumsticks from the thighs and the wings from the breasts.

PORTUGUESE GRILLED CHICKEN WITH SWEETCORN

Who doesn't love peri-peri grilled chicken? We all know fast-food outlets that make awesome versions of this dish but they can be unaffordable for a family of four or five, so I wanted to replicate it at home using a supermarket roast chicken. Peri-peri chicken is all about the smoky flavour, so it's important to use smoked paprika in this recipe. Okay, it's time to pretend you're Cristiano Ronaldo and get ready to blow away your taste buds.

SERVES 4

What you'll need

1 supermarket whole roast chicken
2 x 425 g packets of corn cobbettes

PERI-PERI MARINADE

2 tablespoons smoked paprika
1 teaspoon salt flakes
1 tablespoon garlic powder
2 tablespoons lemon juice
1 tablespoon olive oil
1 tablespoon ground coriander

Now what?

Let's start with the peri-peri marinade. Place the ingredients in a small bowl and stir well to combine. Pop the marinade aside while you prepare the chicken.

Place the roast chicken on a chopping board, breast-side down. Next, we are going to butterfly the chicken. To do this, grab a pair of scissors and cut along either side of the back bone and remove it. Turn the chicken over and gently press to flatten it. Using your fingers, peel the skin off the chicken – don't stress if you can't remove all the skin, it's good either way.

Place a chargrill pan over high heat. Let it heat up while we rock the next part.

Grab your marinade and use a pastry brush to paint, or should I say baste, the chook. Be generous! Flip the chicken over and brush the inside too – the more flavour the better.

Reduce the heat to medium, then add the chicken and cook for about 5 minutes – we want to just caramelise the marinade and not dry out the already-cooked chook. Once you can smell the delicious aromas of the smoked paprika and lemon juice you will automatically do a happy dance. Remove the chicken from the pan and cover with foil to keep warm.

Zap the corn in the microwave according to the packet instructions, then brush with a little of the leftover marinade. Add to the pan and cook for 2–3 minutes.

Serve the chicken on a board whole or cut up into pieces. Surround with the corn and enjoy.

Did you know?

If you don't have a fresh lemon, you can use lime juice or even orange juice instead. In some parts of Portugal they add whisky to the marinade. Be creative and make it your own.

MEXICAN-STYLE CHICKEN & AVO SALSA

I've been making this dish for ten years and, in my opinion, it has one of the best flavour combos: lime, coriander and avocado. When I make it we usually sit in front of the TV and scoop portions into our bowls. All you can hear is crunch, crunch, crunch – I love it! I always add the chilli on the side as my little humans Anela and Kiki would lose it if they ate chilli. There are a few ways you can serve this dish, but I'm going to focus on the fun way to eat it.

SERVES 4

Go grab this stuff

- **1 supermarket whole roast chicken**
- **juice of 1 lime, plus lime wedges to serve**
- **250 g (1 cup) natural yoghurt**
- **1 long red chilli, sliced (optional)**
- **230 g packet of traditional corn chips**

AVO SALSA

- **2 avocados, diced**
- **½ red onion, finely chopped**
- **3 tomatoes, diced**
- **1 bunch of coriander, leaves picked and finely chopped**
- **juice of 2 limes**
- **1 teaspoon salt flakes**

Rock it like this

Using your hands, peel away the chicken skin and discard it. Don't worry if you don't get it all – I sometimes like to leave the skin on for that extra fatty flavour. Remove the chicken meat from the bones and use two forks to shred the meat. Pop the chicken in a bowl and clean your chopping board.

Time to make the avo salsa. Place the avocado, onion, tomato and coriander in a large bowl. Add the lime juice and salt, then drop in the shredded chicken. Give it all a good mix.

Stir the lime juice into the natural yoghurt for extra tang, then transfer to a small serving bowl.

To serve, pile the chicken mixture onto a chopping board and place the lime yoghurt alongside for dipping. Arrange the corn chips around the chicken, or put them in little metal buckets for that semi-fancy look. Top with the chilli (or serve it in a bowl alongside) and add some lime wedges for squeezing over.

Handy hints

If you like, you can replace the corn chips with mini pita breads – simply slice them open and fill with the delicious chicken mixture.

Fresh limes are best for this dish, but you can use lime from a squeezy bottle if you can't get your hands on the real thing.

Any leftovers are ideal for lunch the next day; just serve in a wrap and everyone is super happy. Adding grated cheese is the icing on the cake.

SPEEDY TERIYAKI CHICKEN & RICE

Teriyaki chicken is the bomb. It's sweet and tangy and takes no time at all to prepare.
When I first learned how to make teriyaki sauce I tried it with everything: beef,
chicken, fish, veggies – it's so versatile.

SERVES 4–5

Stuff you gotta get

- 1 supermarket whole roast chicken
- 1 bunch of bok choy, leaves separated
- 2 x 250 g packets of microwave long-grain white rice
- sesame seeds, to serve

TERIYAKI SAUCE

- 3 cm piece of ginger, finely grated
- 3 tablespoons soy sauce
- 3 tablespoons sweet sherry
- 1 tablespoon brown sugar

It's time to do this

Grab a small saucepan and drop in the teriyaki sauce ingredients. Stir over low heat until the sugar is dissolved, then increase the heat to medium and cook for about 5 minutes, until the sauce is slightly thickened. The smell should be filling your kitchen with sweet goodness.

Follow the instructions on page 111 to cut the chicken into eight pieces. Place the chicken in a large baking dish in a single layer and drizzle the teriyaki sauce over it – be as messy as you like.

Crank up the grill to maximum heat and grill the chicken for 3–5 minutes. Remember, we only want to reheat the chicken and caramelise the sauce, so don't leave it in there too long or it will dry out. Remove from the grill, then slice or break up into smaller pieces with your hands.

Meanwhile, blanch the bok choy in boiling water for 1–2 minutes, then drain and set aside.

Microwave the rice according to the packet instructions, then transfer to serving bowls. Top with the bok choy and chicken, and drizzle a little of the teriyaki sauce from the baking dish over everything. Sprinkle with some sesame seeds and you're done!

Bonus stuff

This teriyaki sauce recipe is awesome. I recommend making up a big batch and storing it in portions in the freezer for future use. It will keep for up to 3 months.

'You've gotta try this dish. It's so awesome it made it onto the cover (lol).'

Make simple lettuce cups by filling iceberg or cos lettuce leaves with shredded roast chook, sliced carrot and capsicum, coriander leaves and a drizzle of hoisin sauce. Fresh!

Any leftover Mexican-style Chicken and Avo Salsa (see page 114) works a treat the next day. Add some cheese, lime wedges and mini tortillas and you've got yourself an awesome lunch.

TOO-EASY THAI-STYLE CHICKEN

I absolutely love Thai food, but many of us only think of green curries and satay skewers. The first time I made this Thai-inspired sauce it rocked my world so much that I started using it as a salad dressing and a dip for rice paper rolls. If you've ever eaten street food in Thailand, this recipe will instantly take you there – the smell, the taste … Tuk tuk anyone?

SERVES 4

Grab all of this

2 baby cos lettuces
1 supermarket whole roast chicken
2 x 250 g packets of microwave long-grain white rice
3 tablespoons roasted peanuts, crushed or chopped
coriander leaves, to serve (optional)
1 long red chilli, sliced (optional)

THAI-STYLE SAUCE

4 garlic cloves, crushed
5 sprigs of coriander, very finely chopped (optional)
1 tablespoon palm sugar, grated
1 teaspoon sesame oil
1 tablespoon fish sauce
1 tablespoon soy sauce
1 bird's eye chilli, very finely chopped (optional)

Okay, let's get to it

Separate the lettuce leaves and rinse them thoroughly, then arrange them on a serving platter or chopping board.

Combine the Thai-style sauce ingredients in a small bowl and whisk until the palm sugar dissolves. Remember to taste test to make sure you're happy with the flavour.

Cut the chicken into eight pieces following the instructions on page 111. Place the chicken either on or next to the lettuce in a single layer, then drizzle the sauce over the top, making sure you get in all the nooks and crannies and that every bit of chicken is well coated.

Microwave the rice according to the packet instructions, then transfer to a serving bowl.

Sprinkle the peanuts and coriander (if using) on top of the chicken and lettuce. If you like heat, scatter the sliced chilli over, too. Serve with the rice on the side.

Bonus stuff

Although I've made it optional, the addition of chilli in this Thai-style sauce elevates it to a crazy new level. Give it a go.

The beauty of chicken is that it is just as delicious cold, so you can buy your chicken the night before and store it in the fridge. It's also easier to cut a chicken when it's cold.

SATAY CHICKEN SKEWERS

My girls love chicken skewers; in fact, they love anything on skewers. I guess it's the lollipop vibe, lol. The secret to my satay sauce is the addition of red curry paste. I like to make a big batch of it and store it in portions in the freezer for future use. I really hope you enjoy this recipe, it's one of my faves.

SERVES 4

What you'll need

- 1 supermarket whole roast chicken
- 2 x 250 g packets of microwave long-grain white rice
- 1 Lebanese cucumber, halved, deseeded and sliced into half moons
- 3 spring onions, chopped

SATAY SAUCE

- 1 tablespoon red curry paste
- 80 g smooth peanut butter
- 125 ml (½ cup) coconut cream
- 1 tablespoon soy sauce
- 1 tablespoon palm sugar, grated

Rock it like this

Soak eight bamboo skewers in a large bowl of cold water for 30 minutes. Drain.

To make the satay sauce, grab a small saucepan and add the red curry paste. Cook, stirring, over medium heat for 5 minutes, until it starts to sizzle. Add the rest of the ingredients and keep stirring until the sugar dissolves and the sauce thickens.

Cut the chicken into eight pieces following the instructions on page 111 (try to separate the breast and leg without shredding the chicken). Gently peel the skin off the chicken (or leave it on if you prefer).

We now need to cut the chicken into cubes. Cut each breast into four pieces, then remove the remaining meat from the bones in large chunks and trim into rough cube shapes. Thread the chicken onto the prepared skewers, alternating the breast and leg meat.

Microwave the rice according to the packet instructions, then transfer to a serving bowl. Place the cucumber in a small bowl.

Place the chicken skewers on a tray or platter, spoon over the satay sauce and sprinkle with the spring onion to create a masterpiece. Serve with the rice and cucumber.

More stuff

You don't have to skewer the chicken if you don't have the time – choose your own adventure, just don't change my sauce, okay?

If you want to make up a big batch of satay sauce, simply divide it into portions and store in the freezer for up to 3 months.

NO-KISSING GARLIC CHICKEN WITH ASPARAGUS

Cook this dish when you're in the bad books and there's no chance of kissing anyone, or serve it to the whole family so you won't notice the smell of garlic on each other. I love cooking this dish when it's cold and wintery outside. The garlic butter is so quick to make – it's perfect for when I get home late from work. By the time the kids have set the table the meal is ready to go.

SERVES 4

Grab all of this

1 bunch of asparagus, woody ends trimmed

2 x 250 g packets of microwave long-grain white rice

1 supermarket whole roast chicken

1 teaspoon finely chopped flat-leaf parsley leaves, to serve (optional)

lemon wedges, to serve

GARLIC BUTTER

50 g salted butter

3 tablespoons finely chopped garlic

Now the easy bit

Start with the garlic butter. Grab a large saucepan, add the butter and melt over low heat. Add the garlic and let it gently sizzle for 2–3 minutes until soft. If the heat is too high the butter and garlic will burn and taste bitter, so keep it low and slow. Add the asparagus and cook, tossing in the garlic butter, for 1 minute.

Whack the rice in the microwave and cook according to the packet instructions.

Carve up the chicken as fancy or as rustic as you like and place on a serving board. Add the asparagus, then drizzle the garlic butter over the chicken and asparagus. If you like, peel back some of the skin of the chicken so that the butter melts through and penetrates the meat.

Sprinkle over the parsley (if using) and serve with the rice and lemon wedges for squeezing over. Grab your fork, take a seat and off you go.

Did you know?

I first made this dish using olive oil instead of butter – it was delicious, just saying.

I nearly always serve this with a simple side salad, so it's a good idea to have some washed green leaves in the fridge, ready to go.

This sauce also works wonders with ginger – yummo!

STICKY FINGERS SESAME CHICKEN

Is there anything better than licking the last bit of marinade from your fingers after a delicious meal? There's something so satisfying when I see my daughters Kiki and Anela do just that. When I make my sticky fingers sesame chicken I've been known to lick the plate and even the table if there's any on there. Weirdo, I know! What I love about this recipe is that you can prepare the sauce way in advance – I love to fill old jam jars a few days beforehand and have them ready to go.

SERVES 4

Grab the following

1 supermarket whole roast chicken
4 x 90 g packets of 2-minute noodles
70 g (1 cup) broccoli florets
70 g (1 cup) snow peas, trimmed
1 spring onion, chopped
sesame seeds, to serve

STICKY SESAME SAUCE

175 g (½ cup) honey
3 tablespoons soy sauce
1 tablespoon lime juice
50 g (⅓ cup) sesame seeds

It's time to do this

First things first, remove the chicken from the bag and divide it into eight pieces following the instructions on page 111.

To make the sticky sesame sauce, place the ingredients in a saucepan and whisk over medium–low heat until warmed through. We only want the ingredients to infuse, not boil like lava.

Cook your noodles according to the packet instructions, then drain and set aside.

Put your kettle on to boil. Pop the broccoli and snow peas in a heatproof bowl and cover with the boiling water. Let them sit for 90 seconds, then drain well.

Divide the noodles among four bowls and top each bowl with two pieces of chicken. Add the blanched veggies and spring onion and spoon half the sauce over the top. Sprinkle some sesame seeds over the chicken. Pop the rest of the sauce in small dipping bowls, so everyone can dip their chicken for even more sticky, saucy goodness. You're welcome.

Handy hints

If you add chilli to the sauce it takes on a completely different taste. It's not for everyone but damn it's so good.

You can use low-sodium soy sauce or even sweet soy sauce; it's all about personal preference.

The sticky sesame sauce can be stored in the fridge for up to 1 week, so keep any leftovers for more delicious dipping later in the week.

Roast chicken coated in a sweet and sticky Thai-style sauce? I'll order that for lunch any day! Check out page 121 to see how.

Head to page 122 for my Satay Chicken Skewers recipe. It comes together in no time and is delicious for lunch the next day.

SPANISH-STYLE RICE WITH CHICKEN & CHORIZO

The secret to this recipe is the chorizo; the fat in the sausage flavours the chicken and takes it to the next level. This dish is inspired by Spanish paella with a touch of Macedonia and a lot of love. My local butcher sells the most awesome homemade cured chorizo sausages. Get to know your local butcher and ask their name, then the next time you pop in you can say, 'Hi Bob'. They'll take notice of you and hopefully share some special secret-stash sausages. It works for me.

SERVES 4

Grab the following

1 supermarket whole roast chicken
2 x 250 g packets of microwave long-grain white rice
1 tablespoon olive oil
1 red onion, sliced
3 garlic cloves, sliced
2 chorizo sausages, cut into 1 cm thick slices
1 red capsicum, cut into thin strips
1 yellow capsicum, cut into thin strips
2 fresh jalapenos, finely sliced
125 ml (½ cup) vegetable stock
pinch of salt flakes
1 tablespoon smoked paprika
8 cherry tomatoes, halved

Now what?

Divide the chicken into eight pieces following the instructions on page 111. We are leaving the skin on in this dish, so get ready for an extra cardio session next week (or not). Put the chicken aside.

Microwave the rice according to the packet instructions.

Heat the olive oil in a large frying pan or pot over medium heat. Add the onion and garlic and let the smell fill your kitchen for 2 minutes, then add the chorizo and cook for 3–4 minutes, until the fat is released. Add the rice, red and yellow capsicum and jalapeno and give everything a stir. Pour in the vegetable stock, add the salt and paprika and cook, stirring, for 5 minutes or until the veggie stock thickens and the rice starts to stick to the base of the pan. Lastly, drop in the tomatoes (we want them to remain juicy), add the chicken and gently stir to bring it all together.

I like to serve this in the pan or pot, similar to paella. Crack open a bottle of red wine, sit back and get stuck into this awesomeness (and hope that the kids don't eat all of theirs).

Extra awesome stuff

I use vegetable stock so it doesn't clash with the delicious fat from the chorizo, but you can use any stock you like.

You can swap out the chorizo for normal sausages, but you might need to add more spice or bite.

'If you don't want to share this with the kids, just say it's spicy.'

SUPER-FAST CHICKEN PITAS & TZATZIKI

Who doesn't love street food? It somehow satisfies the soul when you eat from a street stall, especially after a few drinks on a night out. I came up with this recipe to recreate that soulful street food feeling at home. I've also included a quick and easy homemade tzatziki that's super versatile and can be used with loads of other dishes, so screenshot it and share it with your BFF.

SERVES 4

What you'll need

1 supermarket whole roast chicken
1 tablespoon garlic powder
1 teaspoon salt flakes
juice of ½ lemon
2 tablespoons olive oil
8 pita breads or tortillas
½ red onion, finely sliced
2 tomatoes, sliced into rounds
large handful of chopped lettuce

TZATZIKI

1 Lebanese cucumber
3 garlic cloves, crushed
juice of ½ lemon
1 tablespoon olive oil
3 tablespoons chopped mint leaves
250 g (1 cup) natural yoghurt

Now do this

Using your hands, peel off the chicken skin and discard it. If you're doing this job on your own you have the right to sneak a few mouthfuls of chicken as a taste test. Shred the chicken into a large bowl, then add the garlic powder, salt, lemon juice and oil and stir until the chicken is evenly coated.

To make the tzatziki, grate the cucumber onto a few layers of paper towel, then wring them out to remove the excess moisture and drop the cucumber into a bowl. Stir through the garlic, lemon juice, oil, mint and yoghurt and remember to taste test.

Heat a frying pan (or use a chargrill pan with grooves in it for bonus scoring points) over medium–high heat. Working in batches, add the pita breads or tortillas and lightly toast on both sides until warm and soft but not crispy.

Stack the pita breads or tortillas on a serving platter and add individual piles of the chicken, onion, tomato and lettuce, with the tzatziki on the side. Invite your peeps to assemble their own and get stuck in.

Handy hints

The tzatziki can also be used as a dip, so store that one in your memory for future use.

This recipe makes enough for eight pitas, but you can easily double it if friends are coming over. It adds an awesome street food vibe to any social gathering and allows you to socialise rather than slave in the kitchen.

SO-GOOD CAJUN QUINOA CHICKEN

This is somewhat of a surprise dish. I never expected it to be so good that it would make the cut out of the 142 chicken dishes I tested for this book. Okay, it might not have been quite 142 but it must have been close ... This dish is designed to introduce you to the magical world of quinoa. The sultanas add a touch of sweetness, which the kids love. Very rarely are there any leftovers.

SERVES ME (KIDDING, SERVES 4)

Stuff you gotta get

- 2 x 250 g packets of microwave quinoa and brown rice (or use straight microwave quinoa if you prefer)
- 2 tablespoons olive oil
- 3 garlic cloves, crushed
- ½ onion, finely diced
- 1 teaspoon salt flakes
- 3 tablespoons sultanas
- 3 tablespoons chopped coriander leaves, plus extra whole leaves to serve
- 1 supermarket whole roast chicken
- lime wedges, to serve

Time to get cracking

Microwave the quinoa and rice according to the packet instructions.

Heat the olive oil in a frying pan over medium heat, add the garlic and onion and cook for 2–3 minutes, until translucent. Add the quinoa and rice while it's still hot, then stir through the salt, sultanas and chopped coriander.

Cut the chicken into four pieces following the instructions on 111. Do a coin toss to see who in the family gets a breast or leg.

For the Instagram shot, top the quinoa and rice with coriander leaves and arrange some lime wedges artfully nearby. Let people help themselves. You're welcome.

Bonus stuff

If your little peeps don't like to eat off the bone you can shred the chicken instead.

You can pop the chicken under a hot grill for a few minutes if you'd like to crisp it up. However you decide to eat it, make sure you enjoy it and especially the time you've saved.

If you're not a quinoa fan, you can use plain brown or black rice for a similar vibe.

You'll be the envy of the office when you take my Spanish-style Rice with Chicken and Chorizo (see page 130) in for lunch. Next-level flavour but so quick and easy to make!

Tacos, meatballs, burgers and other insanely good (and easy!) mince recipes

MIGHTY MINCE

EVERYDAY TACOS

When I do school pick-up on a Tuesday and I ask Anela and Kiki what they'd like for dinner they will always say tacos. Even if it's not a Tuesday, they'll still ask for tacos. This recipe is so simple and one that Kiki helps me to prepare. Vamos!

SERVES 4

Ingredients you'll need

1 tablespoon olive oil
½ **onion, diced**
2 **garlic cloves, crushed**
500 g beef mince
1 tablespoon smoked paprika
1 teaspoon ground cumin
1 tablespoon salt flakes
½ **teaspoon dried oregano**

TACO TOPPINGS

2 cups shredded iceberg lettuce
1 tomato, sliced into wedges
125 g (1 cup) grated cheddar
125 g can sweetcorn kernels, rinsed
   and drained
1 avocado, sliced
½ **cup coriander leaves**
250 g (1 cup) sour cream
1 lime, cut into wedges
12 mini soft flour tortillas

Time to get cracking

Heat the oil in a large frying pan over medium heat, add the onion and garlic and cook for about 1 minute, until just starting to turn translucent. Add the mince and cook, breaking up any lumps with the back of a wooden spoon, for 4–5 minutes, until browned. Stir through the paprika, cumin, salt and oregano, then add 125 ml (½ cup) of water and stir to combine. Bring to a simmer and cook for 8 minutes.

I like to present the toppings on a large chopping board. Place the lettuce, tomato, cheddar, sweetcorn, avocado and coriander in little bowls on the board and place a serving spoon in each bowl. Spoon the sour cream into a small bowl, squeeze one of the lime wedges over the top and stir, then place the remaining wedges on the board.

Grab a large bowl, add the mince including all the juices from the pan and place it next to the toppings and sour cream.

Warm the tortillas in the microwave according to the packet instructions or for a few seconds each side in a dry frying pan over medium heat. Alternatively, you can turn them into hard taco shells by baking them in a preheated 200°C oven for 6 minutes.

For me, the best thing about making tacos is watching my family assemble them, seeing what toppings they choose and getting sour cream all over their faces. So sit back and watch the seagulls swoop in and go for the attack.

More stuff

I like to use beef mince as it's quick to cook, but you can also use pork, chicken or even turkey mince – just make sure you adjust the cooking time.

You can serve up any taco toppings including store-bought salsa. I always top my own tacos with fresh sliced chilli or a good chilli sauce. Enjoy.

CHEESEBURGER SALAD BOWL

Ridiculously FAST!

Why do we feel bad when we eat cheeseburgers for dinner? It always makes me feel guilty for some reason, so I decided to turn my beloved cheeseburger into an easy salad. Genius, right? This recipe is inspired by healthy poke bowls with the addition of cheeseburger greatness. Are you excited?

SERVES 4

What you'll need

- 1 tablespoon olive oil
- 1 iceberg lettuce, shredded
- 2 tomatoes, finely sliced
- 4 dill pickles, finely sliced lengthways

MEATBALLS

- 500 g pork and veal mince
- 1 tablespoon salt flakes
- 1 teaspoon freshly ground black pepper
- ½ cup smashed-up corn chips (plus extra if needed)
- ½ onion, finely chopped
- 1 egg
- 60 g (½ cup) grated cheddar

SPECIAL SAUCE

- 125 g (½ cup) mayonnaise
- 125 g (½ cup) tomato sauce
- 3 tablespoons pickle juice (from the dill pickle jar)
- 1 tablespoon dijon mustard

Now do this

Let's start with the meatballs. Grab a mixing bowl and drop in the pork and veal mince, salt, pepper, corn chips, onion and egg. Using your hands, mix it to the max and make sure you're happy with the consistency – if the mixture feels too wet or soggy, add a few more smashed corn chips. Divide the mixture into eight even portions and roll them into meatballs. Working with one meatball at a time, use a finger to poke a little hole in the middle and add 2 teaspoons of the grated cheddar (we want the cheese to be trapped in the middle with nowhere to escape). Repeat with the remaining meatballs and cheddar.

Heat the oil in a frying pan over medium heat, add the meatballs and cook, turning frequently, for 8–10 minutes, until browned and cooked through.

To make the special sauce, place all the ingredients in a small bowl and mix well.

Grab four serving bowls and divide the lettuce, tomato and dill pickle among the bowls. Top with the meatballs and drizzle some of the special sauce over everything. How good is that?

Bonus stuff

You will notice that there are no burger buns in this recipe as I wanted to make it low in carbs, for a guilt-free alternative to the classic cheeseburger. If you'd like to include a bread component, add a handful of croutons to each bowl.

I like using pork and veal mince as there's a little more flavour from the pork, but you can also use chicken mince.

POLNETI PEPPERS

'Polneti' is the Macedonian word for 'stuffed', and this recipe is straight from my mum's vault. I used to eat these peppers all the time as a kid and I remember just how satisfying they were. The secret to this recipe is a hot oven, so always give it time to properly preheat. My mum used to serve these with a garden salad and bread to dip into the leftover sauce.

SERVES 4

Grab all of this

2 tablespoons olive oil

1 onion, chopped

500 g pork and veal mince

1 teaspoon salt flakes

1 teaspoon smoked paprika

2 tablespoons Vegeta stock powder (this stuff is the bomb and a must-have in the pantry)

1 teaspoon dried mint

400 g can crushed tomatoes

200 g long-grain white rice

15 long red or green bullhorn peppers

250 ml (1 cup) vegetable stock

TO SERVE

crusty bread

garden salad

Let's rock

Preheat the oven to 200°C.

Heat the oil in a large frying pan over medium heat. Add the onion and cook for 5–6 minutes, until translucent, then add the pork and veal mince, salt, paprika, Vegeta and mint and cook, breaking up any lumps of mince with the back of a wooden spoon, for 10 minutes or until the mince is browned. Add 750 ml (3 cups) of water, the tomatoes and rice and stir well to combine. Bring the mixture to a simmer and cook for 8–10 minutes, until the rice is just cooked through.

Meanwhile, remove the stalks from the peppers and use a spoon to scrape out the seeds (don't stress if you leave some behind).

Now it's time to start stuffing – I find that a large spoon is the way to go. Fill the peppers with the mince and rice mixture, then line them up next to each other in a large baking dish. Pour over the stock, transfer to the oven and cook for 15–20 minutes, until the peppers are soft.

Serve the stuffed peppers with crusty bread and a fresh garden salad. They also taste amazing reheated the next day.

Handy hints

You can use chicken mince instead of pork and veal mince, but make sure it's cooked through before adding the rice to the pan.

Traditionally, this recipe uses dried parsley instead of mint, but I find that mint adds a touch of freshness.

I also love serving these peppers on top of the crusty bread. The juices seep into the bread, which you can then eat afterwards – it's seriously awesome.

You don't have to wait for Tuesdays to enjoy tacos! Head to page 140 for my Everyday Taco recipe and find out how it's done.

CHILL-OUT CON CARNE

Chill out and eat my chilli con carne. It's simple and delicious, and my girls love that I pop it in a wrap for them for school the next day. When I used to make chilli con carne on my own I would crank up the spice level to EXTREME, but I had to tone it down once my girls came along. I usually serve it with rice, but you can also toss it through spaghetti, spoon it on top of corn chips to make nachos or even make a Mexican-inspired lasagne.

SERVES 4

Stuff you gotta get

2 tablespoons olive oil
1 onion, chopped
4 garlic cloves, chopped
500 g beef mince
2 x 400 g cans red kidney beans, rinsed and drained
2 x 400 g cans crushed tomatoes
1 tablespoon salt flakes
1 tablespoon smoked paprika
1 teaspoon ground cinnamon
2 red capsicums, roughly chopped
2 x 250 g packets of microwave long-grain white rice

TO SERVE
natural yoghurt
chopped coriander leaves
lime wedges

Now what?

Heat the oil in your largest frying pan over medium heat. Add the onion and garlic and cook for 3–4 minutes, until translucent, then add the beef mince and cook, breaking up any lumps with the back of a wooden spoon, for 7–8 minutes, until browned.

Add the kidney beans, tomatoes, salt, paprika and cinnamon and stir until well combined. Add the capsicum, then simmer for about 20 minutes, until the mixture is reduced and thick.

Cook the microwave rice according to the packet instructions and divide among four bowls. Spoon the chilli con carne on top, then add a dollop of natural yoghurt and a few chopped coriander leaves. Serve with lime wedges on the side.

But wait, there's more!

You can easily swap the rice for corn chips to make the ultimate nachos platter. Grate some cheese over the top and pop under a hot grill until just melted.

If you want to make a vegan chilli con carne, ditch the mince and use a 400 g can of drained and rinsed chickpeas instead. Swap the natural yoghurt for mashed avocado and you're good to go!

STICKY PORK NOODLES

I have a massive sweet tooth, so when I eat sticky–sweet Asian dishes I feel like I'm doubling up by having a sweet main followed by dessert. Oh well, win–win. This is one of the simplest recipes in the book. It's a cracking midweek meal that takes no time at all to cook. The secret is the pork, which works well with sweeter sauces and marinades.

SERVES 4

What you'll need

3 x 90 g packets of 2-minute
  noodles

2 tablespoons sesame oil

1 tablespoon grated ginger

1 tablespoon grated garlic

500 g pork mince

300 g packet of mixed Asian
  vegetables

80 ml (⅓ cup) hoisin sauce

80 ml (⅓ cup) soy sauce

coriander leaves, to serve

Time to get cracking

First, cook the 2-minute noodles according to the packet instructions. You probably won't believe this, but it only takes 2 minutes to cook them. Drain and set aside.

If you have a wok, it's time to wok 'n' roll; otherwise, grab a large frying pan. Add the sesame oil and heat over high heat, then add the ginger, garlic and pork mince, breaking up any lumps with the back of a wooden spoon. Move the mixture around quickly, tossing and flipping the ingredients like they do in Chinese restaurants. Cook the pork for 5–6 minutes, until white, then add the vegetables, hoisin sauce and soy sauce and keep stirring.

Now grab a drink and take a seat ... just kidding! Add the noodles to the wok or frying pan and flip or stir them through – the smell should be filling your kitchen and I'm sure you've already tried some. Nice, hey?

Divide the sticky pork noodles among serving bowls and scatter some coriander leaves over the top.

More stuff

I use 2-minute noodles because they're quick and easy, but you can use rice noodles or any other noodles that you have in your pantry. You can also use honey instead of hoisin sauce if you don't like spice.

Pre-packaged Asian veggies make this dish super easy, but you can add your own choice of fresh veggies if you prefer.

'Robot-dance level goodness
right here guys.'

MEATBALL PARMIGIANA

Who doesn't love a good parma? This dish is just like a chicken parma but with meatballs! It's best served with a leafy green salad to help balance the heaviness of the cheese and tomato sauce, which I love dipping the baguette into. Trust me, this is a soon-to-be family favourite that the kids will ask for again and again.

SERVES 4

Stuff you gotta get

2 tablespoons olive oil
1 onion, finely diced
4 garlic cloves, crushed
500 g pork and veal mince
2 eggs
50 g (½ cup) dried breadcrumbs
3 tablespoons grated parmesan
2 x 400 g cans crushed tomatoes
300 g (2 cups) grated mozzarella

TO SERVE

crusty baguette
leafy green salad
basil leaves

Now do this

Crank the oven to 180°C.

Grab a baking dish and add the oil, onion and garlic. Set aside.

Now let's make the meatballs. Place the mince, one egg and half the breadcrumbs in a large bowl. Using your hands, squeeze the ingredients together until completely combined.

Whisk the remaining egg in a bowl and combine the remaining breadcrumbs and the parmesan on a plate.

The next steps go like this: roll the mince mixture into roughly golf ball–sized meatballs, dip them into the beaten egg, then roll in the parmesan breadcrumbs to coat. As you finish rolling each meatball, pop it neatly in the baking dish. Once all the meatballs are made, pour the crushed tomatoes into the base of the dish and over the meatballs. Sprinkle the mozzarella on top and whack it in the oven for 20–30 minutes, until the meatballs are cooked through and the cheese is golden and bubbling.

Meanwhile, cut the baguette into thick slices and pop them on a serving board in the middle of the table, along with a leafy green salad.

To serve, scatter over some basil leaves, drop a serving spoon into the baking dish and bring it to the table. Let the family attack it like a bunch of hungry seagulls attacking a chip.

Did you know?

You can use any mince you like in this recipe. If you prefer your meatballs crunchy, crisp them up in 1 tablespoon of olive oil in a frying pan over medium–high heat for 4–5 minutes before adding them to the baking dish.

Make up a big batch of my Meatball Parmigiana (see the previous page for the recipe) then pop any leftovers in a bread roll the next day. Ridiculously good.

Over sandwiches? Try my Sticky Pork Noodles (see page 150) instead. There'll be no turning back.

FAST & FRESH VIETNAMESE MEATBALL SALAD

I love everything about Vietnamese cuisine and culture and I can't wait to get back there to learn more. I especially love their use of fresh herbs and delicious marinades and dressings. Here is a simplified version of the popular dish, *bun cha*, which is absolutely off the charts.

SERVES 4

Grab the following

500 g pork mince

2 tablespoons fish sauce

2 lemongrass stalks, white part only, finely chopped

2 garlic cloves, crushed

3 tablespoons sugar

4–5 spring onions, finely sliced

1 teaspoon salt flakes

2 tablespoons vegetable oil

VIETNAMESE NOODLE SALAD

400 g vermicelli rice noodles

1 carrot, julienned

1 Lebanese cucumber, halved lengthways, deseeded and sliced into half moons

1 long red chilli, deseeded and julienned (optional)

6–8 lettuce leaves of your choice, roughly chopped

⅓ cup coriander leaves

Vietnamese Dressing (see page 31)

Time to get cracking

Grab a bowl and drop in the mince, fish sauce, lemongrass, garlic, sugar, spring onion and salt. Using your hands, give it a good mix and make sure all the ingredients are well combined.

I like to make traditional-looking Vietnamese meatballs. Spoon a tablespoon of the mince mixture into your hand and form it into a flattish, rounded meatball that's about half the size of your palm. Set aside on a plate and repeat with the remaining mince mixture to make about 12 meatballs.

Heat the vegetable oil in a large frying pan over medium–high heat. Working in batches, cook the meatballs for about 3 minutes each side, until they are caramelised and cooked through.

To make the noodle salad, cook the vermicelli noodles according to the packet instructions, then drain and rinse under running water until cold (you can also cook the noodles ahead of time and store them in the fridge if you prefer). Thoroughly drain the noodles, then transfer to a salad bowl.

Add the carrot, cucumber, chilli (if using), lettuce and coriander to the noodles. Add some of the Vietnamese dressing and toss well to combine. Place the meatballs on top of the salad and serve, while shaking your head in amazement at how much of a flavour punch this dish has.

Bonus stuff

Pork is predominately used in Vietnam for these meatballs, but you can also use chicken or turkey mince in this recipe, plus cold chicken tastes awesome which means you'll have an amazing lunch the next day.

PIRINSKA 8 (AKA MACEDONIAN BAKED BEANS WITH MEATBALLS)

This dish is special to me. The name Pirinska 8 was my grandmother's street address back in Macedonia. I've dedicated this recipe to her and her beautiful warmth and contagious smile that recharged my heart and soul every time I saw her. This is something of a hybrid recipe, based on the traditional Macedonian dish, *tavche gravche*, but with an Aussie twist and a hint of Italian. Gotta love our multicultural country.

SERVES 4–6

Go grab this stuff
1 tablespoon vegetable oil
4 x 400 g cans cannellini beans
400 g can diced tomatoes
1 onion, finely chopped
4 garlic cloves, finely chopped
1 teaspoon salt flakes
1 tablespoon smoked paprika
4 long red or green chillies
1 tablespoon chopped mint leaves
crusty bread, to serve

PORK MEATBALLS
500 g pork mince
3 tablespoons chopped mint leaves
3 tablespoons chopped flat-leaf
   parsley leaves
1 egg
2 tablespoons grated parmesan
1 tablespoon garlic powder
1 teaspoon salt flakes

Now the easy bit
Preheat the oven to 190°C.

Let's make the pork meatballs first. Drop the ingredients into a large bowl and use your hands to mix and squeeze the ingredients until really well combined. Roll the mixture into palm-sized balls and set aside on a plate.

Place a frying pan over high heat and add the vegetable oil. Sear the meatballs for about 1 minute each side until browned (we don't want to cook them through).

Tip the cannellini beans (including the liquid in the cans) and the tomatoes into a large baking dish. Scatter over the onion and garlic and sprinkle with the salt and smoked paprika. Give it a good mix to combine, then top with the meatballs and whole chillies so they look super cool. Pop the dish in the oven for about 20 minutes or until the liquid thickens.

Sprinkle the mint over the top and get ready to fill your soul. I like to add a serving spoon to the dish and invite everyone to help themselves. Serve with crusty bread for mopping up the tomatoey sauce.

But wait, there's more!
You can use pork chops, beef cheeks or even raw prawns instead of the pork meatballs; just remember to adjust the cooking time accordingly.

Any canned beans will work well in this dish – try kidney beans, black beans or even borlotti beans. Let your imagination run wild!

Damn-good beef, lamb and pork dishes that will earn you legend status in the kitchen

CALLING ALL MEAT LOVERS

VIETNAMESE LEMONGRASS PORK & RICE

Nothing screams Vietnamese food like lemongrass, and in this recipe it brings such a knock-out flavour to an incredibly simple marinade. I've tried different versions of this pork and rice dish in the various regions of Vietnam I have visited. This is my interpretation, combining all the Vietnamese flavours that I love. Ideally you need to marinate the pork overnight, but if you're short on time, an hour or two will also work. It's even better for lunch the next day.

SERVES 4

Go grab this stuff

- 1 kg pork sirloin steaks
- 450 g packet of microwave long-grain white rice
- ½ iceberg lettuce, shredded
- 1 tomato, chopped
- 1 Lebanese cucumber, halved lengthways, deseeded and sliced into half moons

VIETNAMESE MARINADE

- 3 tablespoons brown sugar
- 2 tablespoons soy sauce
- 2 tablespoons fish sauce
- 3 tablespoons vegetable oil
- 2 lemongrass stalks, white part only, finely chopped
- 2 tablespoons minced garlic
- 2 tablespoons sliced shallots

Rock it like this

Grab a small bowl and drop in all the Vietnamese marinade ingredients. Give it a good mix, and a taste test – it should taste sour and sweet.

Place the pork steaks in a large baking dish in a single layer and pour over most of the marinade, reserving about 60 ml (¼ cup). Transfer the pork and leftover marinade to the fridge and leave to marinate overnight or for at least 1 hour.

Heat a large frying pan over medium heat. Take the pork steaks out of the marinade and cook for 3–4 minutes. Flip the steaks over, pour in the marinade from the dish and continue to cook for 4 minutes, until the steaks are cooked through.

Microwave the rice according to the packet instructions.

Divide the rice among four plates, position the pork steaks on top of the rice and drizzle over the reserved marinade. Place the lettuce, tomato and cucumber next to the pork. Grab a fork and take a seat, dinner's ready!

BARBECUED VEGEMITE BEEF RIBS

'WHAT?!' I hear you say. Vegemite is as Aussie as it gets, so I decided to use it to make barbecued ribs. When I first made this dish I added way too much Vegemite, but after a few attempts I have mastered the marinade and I love it, big time. The flavours are actually really complex and taste so damn good. The ribs don't need to marinate, which means they take less time to prepare.

SERVES JUST ME … KIDDING, SERVES 4

Ingredients you'll need

2 x 1 kg racks of beef ribs
425 g packet of corn cobbettes
40 g salted butter
2 teaspoons salt flakes
350 g packet of coleslaw
Coleslaw Dressing (see page 30)

VEGEMITE MARINADE

80 ml (⅓ cup) vegetable oil
1 tablespoon Vegemite
2 tablespoons boiling water
1 teaspoon sesame seeds
1 tablespoon smoked paprika
2 teaspoons garlic powder
1 tablespoon honey

It's time to do this

Fire up the barbecue grill on high.

Place the Vegemite marinade ingredients in a bowl and whisk with a fork until smooth. Using a pastry brush or your fingers (pop gloves on first), glaze the beef ribs with the marinade until they are evenly coated.

When the barbecue is hot and ready, pop the ribs on the grill and turn down the heat slightly so they cook evenly without burning. Cook for 8 minutes each side or until cooked through.

While the ribs are cooking, zap the corn in the microwave according to the packet instructions, then add to the grill. Dab the butter over the corn and sprinkle with the salt – we only want to briefly char it as it's already cooked.

Drop the coleslaw in a serving bowl and toss through some of the coleslaw dressing.

Baste the cooked ribs with any remaining marinade and leave to rest, covered, while you set the table. Place the corn in a serving bowl on the table, along with the coleslaw.

You can either slice the beef into individual ribs or serve the racks whole and invite everyone to help themselves. Enjoy with the corn and slaw.

Extra awesome stuff

Personally I wouldn't change this recipe but if you do, don't ditch the Vegemite. It's what makes the marinade taste so amazing, and essentially replaces traditional soy sauce and salt. This marinade is also amazing with pork ribs.

EASY-AS PORK CHOPS & APPLE SLAW

This has to be the easiest recipe in this book. I almost feel bad for including it, but no one you serve it to needs to know, nor will they notice when they taste how delicious it is. Sometimes I just chill out in the kitchen with a glass of wine while my family thinks I'm working hard preparing their dinner. Pork and apple is a classic pairing. Here, the acidity of the apple and the sweetness of the dressing balances the savoury pork to make a marriage that gets my blessing any time of the year.

SERVES 4

Grab the following

600 g packet of coleslaw
1 green apple, julienned
½ red onion, finely sliced (optional; leave this out if the coleslaw already contains onion)
Coleslaw Dressing (see page 30)
1 tablespoon vegetable oil
1 kg pork loin chops
1 teaspoon salt flakes
1 teaspoon freshly ground black pepper
lemon wedges, to serve

Now do this

Combine the coleslaw, apple and onion (if using) in a large bowl. Add 3 tablespoons of the coleslaw dressing and toss together.

Place a frying pan over medium heat and add the oil. Season the pork with the salt and pepper, then add to the pan and cook for 4 minutes each side or until cooked through.

Divide the slaw among four plates and whack a few pork chops on top. Drizzle a tablespoon of coleslaw dressing over the pork and serve straight away with lemon wedges for squeezing over.

More stuff

I told you this recipe was easy! There's no need to change a thing, but if you want to make your own coleslaw from scratch you can. I just prefer the simplicity of using pre-cut vegetables, as it means I can have dinner on the table in next to no time.

LAMB CUTLETS WITH HOMEMADE CHIPS

I love cooking lamb cutlets as much as my girls love eating them. They get excited when they see potatoes come out of the pantry and lamb cutlets from the fridge. It means that dinner is going to be awesome. Please note that my chips are next level; I cook them in an air fryer but if you don't have one you can bake them in the oven.

SERVES 4

What you'll need

8 medium–large red royale potatoes
2 tablespoons olive oil
1 tablespoon Vegeta stock powder
12 lamb cutlets
juice of 1 lemon
1 teaspoon dried oregano
1 teaspoon salt flakes

Now what?

Crank up your air fryer or preheat the oven to 180°C.

Peeling potatoes sucks, so you have two choices: get the kids to do it or don't peel them and leave the skins on. Cut the spuds into 1 cm wide chips, then pop them in a bowl, add 1 tablespoon of the oil and the Vegeta stock powder and toss the chips until they're evenly coated. Transfer to a large baking tray.

If using an air fryer, cook the chips at 180°C for 20 minutes. Alternatively, transfer to the oven and cook for 40 minutes.

Heat the remaining oil in a large frying pan over medium heat. Add the lamb cutlets and cook for 2½ minutes each side or until cooked to your liking. Remove from the pan and rest, covered, for a couple of minutes.

Pop the lamb cutlets in a large bowl and dress with the lemon juice, oregano and salt – we want them to be glistening! Serve the cutlets with the homemade chips and sit back while your family go crazy for them.

But wait, there's more!

You can swap out the lamb cutlets for chicken drumsticks, but the chicken will take longer to cook. The combination of lemon juice and oregano is a winner, and you can use it on any protein, including fish.

My Vietnamese Lemongrass Pork (see page 162) is a little sweet, a little sour and totally delicious. It's even better for lunch the next day.

Slice leftover chops or steak into bite-sized pieces and include a little fork for your kids to use. Add some fruit and veg for colour and crunch and away you go!

BEEF BURRITO CONES

This is a special recipe that's a little bit a cheeky. My girls think it's a burrito in the form of an ice cream. Technically, it's a combination of Mexican-style beef with rice and melted cheese wrapped up in mini tortilla cones. I add rice to the base of each cone to resemble the chocolate in the bottom of a Drumstick ice cream. I then fill the cones with the remaining ingredients, allowing the delicious juices to soak into the rice.

SERVES 4

Ingredients you'll need

1 tablespoon olive oil

520 g beef sizzle steaks, sliced into thin strips

1 red capsicum, sliced

1 green capsicum, sliced

1 red onion, sliced

2 tablespoons smoked paprika

1 tablespoon salt flakes

1 tablespoon garlic powder

2 x 250 g packets of microwave long-grain white rice

12 mini soft flour tortillas

125 g (1 cup) grated cheddar

TO SERVE

coriander leaves

finely chopped bird's eye chilli (optional)

natural yoghurt

Now do this

Heat the oil in a large frying pan over medium heat, add the sizzle steak and sear for 1 minute each side. Add the capsicum and onion and cook for 2–3 minutes, until starting to soften, then add the smoked paprika, salt, garlic powder and 3 tablespoons of water. Stir like crazy and cook for 2–3 minutes, until the water evaporates. Remove the pan from the heat and set aside.

Preheat the oven to 200°C. Line a baking dish with baking paper.

Cook the microwave rice according to the packet instructions.

Working with one tortilla at a time, fold a tortilla into an ice cream cone shape and hold it upright in one hand. Add 1 tablespoon of rice to the base of the cone and top with 2 tablespoons of the steak and capsicum mixture. Secure the end of the cone with a toothpick and gently lay it in the baking dish. Repeat with the remaining tortillas, rice and steak and capsicum mixture until you have a line-up of sleeping ice cream cones in the baking dish.

Sprinkle the grated cheddar over the top and whack them in the oven for 10–15 minutes, until the cheese is nicely melted.

Scatter the coriander and chilli (if using) over the top of the cones, add a drizzle of yoghurt and serve.

Bonus stuff

You can use a supermarket whole roast chicken instead of steak or even canned beans for a vegetarian version.

For an even healthier dinner, try using black rice instead of white rice.

Most cuts of beef will work in this recipe as long as they are finely sliced.

PORTERHOUSE, PARMESAN CHIPS & CORN RIBS

This is my homemade steakhouse recipe that never fails. The smell of buttery steak
will fill the kitchen, along with the aroma of the chips and sweetcorn in the air fryer.
Is there anything better? If you have an air fryer this dish only takes 20 minutes to make,
but don't worry, you can also cook the chips and corn in the oven. It's time to
sharpen your knife and get cracking.

SERVES 4

Grab the following

**500 g red royale potatoes, peeled
and cut into 1 cm thick chips**

80 ml (⅓ cup) olive oil

2 tablespoons salt flakes

3 sweetcorn cobs

1 tablespoon smoked paprika

80 g salted butter

3 garlic cloves, peeled

3 x 200–250 g porterhouse steaks

2 sprigs of rosemary

3 tablespoons grated parmesan

Let's rock

If you don't have an air fryer, preheat your oven to 200°C.

Place the potato on a baking tray and drizzle over 2 tablespoons
of the oil, along with 1 tablespoon of the salt (I like my chips salty,
so feel free to use less salt if you prefer). Toss to combine.

Cut the sweetcorn lengthways through the core, making sure
each corn rib has a little core attached to keep the kernels
together. Rub 1 tablespoon of the oil over the corn and sprinkle
with the smoked paprika. Add them to the tray with the potato.

If using an air fryer, crank it to 180°C and cook for 20 minutes.
Alternatively, transfer to the oven and cook for 30 minutes, or until
the chips and corn ribs are golden and crispy.

Meanwhile, heat the remaining oil in a large frying pan over high
heat. When the oil starts to smoke, add half the butter and let it
melt. Add the garlic cloves and steaks and cook for 2 minutes,
then flip the steaks over, add the remaining butter and salt, along
with the rosemary sprigs, and continue to cook for 2 minutes,
basting the steaks with the melted butter. The steaks will be
medium–rare, so feel free to cook them for longer if your family
prefers them a little more well done. Remove the steaks from the
pan and rest, covered, for 3–4 minutes. Don't discard the buttery
juices in the pan!

Remove the chips and corn ribs from the air fryer or oven and
divide among serving plates. Scatter the parmesan over the hot
chips and drizzle the corn ribs with the juices from the pan. Slice
up the steak and transfer to the plates. Time to dig in.

Did you know?

You can swap the steaks for chicken, turkey, lamb or pork.
The buttery garlic and rosemary flavour will take any protein
to the next level, just remember to adjust the cooking time.

BEEF & CRISPY NOODLE LETTUCE CUPS

I recently did an online collaboration with a noodle company to pimp up their 2-minute noodles. They asked me to write two recipes, but I was so inspired I ended up writing ten. This dish was an absolute winner and my girls go nuts for it (except Anela, she's allergic to certain nuts). It's time to reveal this bad boy.

SERVES 4–5

Stuff you gotta get

1 tablespoon sesame oil

5 x 120–150 g beef sizzle steaks

1 teaspoon salt flakes

1 teaspoon freshly ground black pepper

90 g packet of 2-minute noodles

2 x 250 g packets of microwave long-grain white rice

4 baby cos lettuces, leaves separated

2 tomatoes, sliced into wedges

1 continental cucumber, halved lengthways and sliced on an angle

coriander leaves, to serve

Vietnamese Dressing (see page 31)

Okay, let's get to it

Heat the sesame oil in a frying pan over medium–high heat. Add the steaks, season with the salt and pepper and cook for 1 minute each side. Transfer the steaks to a plate, cover and leave to rest.

Preheat the oven grill to high.

Cook the 2-minute noodles according to the packet instructions, then drain and transfer to a baking tray. Place the tray under the grill for 5 minutes, until the noodles are crisp and golden brown. Transfer the noodles to a bowl, leave to cool slightly, then break them into pieces with your hands – go gently as you don't want to turn them into powder!

Cook the rice according to the packet instructions, then transfer to a large serving bowl. Place the lettuce leaves on a board, ready to fill.

Slice the steaks into thin strips and add them to the lettuce cups, followed by the tomato, cucumber and crispy noodles. Top with a few coriander leaves, drizzle with the Vietnamese dressing (I like a lot!) and serve with the rice.

'Just watch these get devoured as soon as they hit the table.'

Beef Burrito Cones (see page 173) are guaranteed to bring a smile to your little humans' faces when they open their lunchbox.

Flip back a page to find out how to make these Beef and Crispy Noodle Lettuce Cups. Keep all the leftover ingredients in separate containers overnight (no need to refrigerate the noodles), then make them up fresh in the morning so they don't go soggy.

ITALIAN BEEF STIR-FRY

When I first discussed this recipe idea with my sister Suzy, I didn't know which direction to take it in. I initially thought of an Asian-style noodle dish with Mediterranean flavours, and then I landed on the idea of doing an 'Italian stir-fry'. Sound confusing? Maybe, but trust me, I have fine-tuned this dish to knock your socks off.

SERVES 4

Grab all of this

500 g dried fettuccine

3 tablespoons extra-virgin olive oil

1 onion, chopped

3 garlic cloves, finely chopped

6 x 120–150 g beef sizzle steaks

1 tablespoon salt flakes

1 teaspoon freshly ground
black pepper

8 cherry tomatoes, halved

3 tablespoons finely chopped basil
leaves (optional)

1 long red chilli, finely sliced
(optional)

It's time to do this

Bring a large saucepan of salted water to the boil over high heat, add the fettuccine and cook according to the packet instructions, until al dente.

While the pasta is cooking, heat 1 tablespoon of the oil in a large frying pan over medium heat. Add the onion and garlic and cook for 3–4 minutes, until translucent, then transfer to a bowl.

Add the steaks to the pan, season with the salt and pepper and cook for 1 minute each side. Transfer to a plate and let them rest.

Finally, drop the tomatoes into the pan and cook for about 2 minutes – we want to slightly char them without overcooking.

Drain the pasta and add it to the pan with the tomato. Increase the heat to medium–high and add the remaining oil, along with the onion and garlic. Slice the steaks into 2–3 cm wide strips, then add them to the pan and stir to coat the pasta until it's glistening. Serve straight away, topped with basil and chilli, if desired.

Handy hints

You can also make this dish with a supermarket whole roast chicken – the key element is really the simple flavours of the extra-virgin olive oil, garlic and tomatoes. Make sure you don't swap them out.

Conversion charts

Measuring cups and spoons may vary slightly from one country to another, but the difference is generally not enough to affect a recipe. All cup and spoon measures are level.

One Australian metric measuring cup holds 250 ml (8 fl oz), one Australian tablespoon holds 20 ml (4 teaspoons) and one Australian metric teaspoon holds 5 ml. North America, New Zealand and the UK use a 15 ml (3-teaspoon) tablespoon.

Length

Metric	Imperial
3 mm	⅛ inch
6 mm	¼ inch
1 cm	½ inch
2.5 cm	1 inch
5 cm	2 inches
18 cm	7 inches
20 cm	8 inches
23 cm	9 inches
25 cm	10 inches
30 cm	12 inches

Liquid measures

One American pint	One Imperial pint
500 ml (16 fl oz)	600 ml (20 fl oz)

Cup	Metric	Imperial
⅛ cup	30 ml	1 fl oz
¼ cup	60 ml	2 fl oz
⅓ cup	80 ml	2½ fl oz
½ cup	125 ml	4 fl oz
⅔ cup	160 ml	5 fl oz
¾ cup	180 ml	6 fl oz
1 cup	250 ml	8 fl oz
2 cups	500 ml	16 fl oz
2¼ cups	560 ml	20 fl oz
4 cups	1 litre	32 fl oz

Dry measures

The most accurate way to measure dry ingredients is to weigh them. However, if using a cup, add the ingredient loosely to the cup and level with a knife; don't compact the ingredient unless the recipe requests 'firmly packed'.

Metric	Imperial
15 g	½ oz
30 g	1 oz
60 g	2 oz
125 g	4 oz (¼ lb)
185 g	6 oz
250 g	8 oz (½ lb)
375 g	12 oz (¾ lb)
500 g	16 oz (1 lb)
1 kg	32 oz (2 lb)

Oven temperatures

Celsius	Fahrenheit
100°C	200°F
120°C	250°F
150°C	300°F
160°C	325°F
180°C	350°F
200°C	400°F
220°C	425°F

Celsius	Gas mark
110°C	¼
130°C	½
140°C	1
150°C	2
170°C	3
180°C	4
190°C	5
200°C	6
220°C	7
230°C	8
240°C	9
250°C	10

Thank you!

Mary Small: Without you none of this would have happened. You have given me and my family so much, and your vision and belief in me is something I will always treasure. You literally are the Bestest Publisher in the Universe and thank you for making me an author dad dude. Love you lots.

Jane Winning: When you have Winning as a surname there's no doubt you're on a good thing. As senior editor you've kept me to a light schedule, on time all the time. I love how you operate and your guidance is the secret to my success. Thank you way too much! *Muchas gracias, señorita.*

Lucy Heaver: The editor extraordinaire. I'd add mistakes to my recipes just to keep you on your toes. Lol. Your experience and know-how gave me the confidence that all my grammar would be on point. Ha ha ha. You honestly rock, Shakespeare style.

Kirby Armstrong: You are the layout guru; it is magical the way you have designed my book. This is book number three with you and I couldn't imagine working with anyone else. I appreciate your unique skill and industry know-how to make my book look so good.

Nikole Ramsay: This is the second book that you've photographed for me and the way you capture the dishes is next level, while your kind, gentle soul gave me so much comfort during production. It's rare that I meet people like you and I consider you a friend rather than the best photographer ever. Love you.

Karina van de Pol and The KO Creative Studio: Your styling certainly elevated my recipes to make them book-worthy and watching you rock out in the best studio was next level. Thank you for using every bit of your skill and super powers to make my job so much easier. You are a food stylist extraordinaire, now can you do anything with my look? (Lol.)

Joe Pratt: Chef man. Dude, you rock, helping me to deliver the best dishes I possibly could on set is something I will never forget. Laughing and rocking out to my music is something I will treasure for a long time. You've got the skills to pay the bills. You have elevated me as a dad cook and I'll never forget that.

Mum: You have inspired me in many ways. Your unconditional love and support is entrenched deep in my heart. You have taught me so much about life and how to truly love someone. Your warmth has sparked a fire in me that will always burn. I love you more than you'll ever know.

Dad: It's been over 25 years since you left this world and there's not a minute that you don't cross my mind, whether it's looking in the mirror and seeing how much I look like you or the mannerisms that I've inherited from you. I love your different ways and how much you loved Mum. You're my hero and I miss you so much.

Suzy: My big sister, you're a phenomenal cook and I love how much you inspire a lot of my recipes. I love our daily chats and the love for your family radiates so much. You are very inspiring to me and, as your little brother, I am super proud that you are my sister, even though you used to push me off the couch when I was a toddler.

Vince and the Boys: Bro, Lochs and Julian, you guys are legendary, wise, cool and funny like your uncle. I love how my sister has raised you, and you too, Vince (lol). I'm very proud of the men you have become and I love how you rock to your own beat. Thank you for being next-level humans.

Warren: My best mate and brother. The way you elevate me is amazing; hanging with you inspires me to grow and see the world differently. I love how you have proved to me that vegans can be cool and next-level humans. I love every single one of our nights out and our trips and the 50-euro sausages in France. We're really close, but not as close as you, me and two euro. Brothers for life.

Kiara: Daddy's little girl, you are my little mini me. The way you emulate me in the kitchen and the recipes you create from scratch are so amazing to watch. You are one of the most caring peeps I know and when we rock out in the car singing Lil Peep songs I'm actually storing those moments in my memory to treasure. You have no idea how much you inspire me to do what I do. I love you, Kiki.

Anela: My big girl, you've blossomed in a way that has taught me so much. You are very witty and empathetic towards others and causes. I love who you are and how much you fight for what's right in this world. You are beyond what I could have ever have hoped for. Your subtle criticism of some of my recipe creations is super sweet. I love your heart and your beautiful nature.

Marina: Twenty years of marriage and you still make my heart skip a beat. I love how much you are like your mum; her soul and beautiful ways are embedded in you. Behind every successful man is a woman guiding that man – you have shown me the way and have supported me in many ways. You're my Ms Universe. Love you lots, even when you are showing me how to stack the dishwasher.

Baba Dobrica: My mother-in-law, thank you for your warmth and always making me feel welcome. Your beautiful ways will always be treasured and I am so glad I got to tell you how grateful I am for the beautiful daughter you raised. You are one of a kind, and Anela and Kiki are lucky to have had you in their lives. We will love and miss you forever.

Music: Music is a massive part of my life and I have to mention Eddie Vedder, my future husband. I grew up with his music and his lyrics inspired me in my younger days, with songs like 'Release' saving me from so much pain. I have only recently discovered Lil Peep's music, but I haven't felt such realness since Kurt Cobain. Music is often playing in the kitchen while I cook and I love getting lost within lyrics and food, so thank you!

Index

Pan Macmillan acknowledges the Traditional Custodians of country throughout Australia and their connections to lands, waters and communities. We pay our respect to Elders past and present and extend that respect to all Aboriginal and Torres Strait Islander peoples today. We honour more than sixty thousand years of storytelling, art and culture.

A Plum book

First published in 2022 by
Pan Macmillan Australia Pty Limited
Level 25, 1 Market Street,
Sydney, NSW 2000, Australia

Level 3, 112 Wellington Parade,
East Melbourne, VIC 3002, Australia

Design and typesetting by Kirby Armstrong
Edited by Lucy Heaver
Index by Helena Holmgren
Photography by Nikole Ramsay
Prop and food styling by Karina van de Pol
Food preparation by George Georgievski and Joseph Pratt
Colour reproduction by Splitting Image Colour Studio
Printed and bound in China by 1010 Printing International Limited

A CIP catalogue record for this book is available from the National Library of Australia.

The publisher would like to thank Stuck On You for their generosity in providing props for the book.

10 9 8 7 6 5 4 3 2 1